ALCOHOLISM
Its Causes and Cure

A New Handbook

ALCOHOLISM
Its Causes and Cure

A New Handbook

Harry Milt

Charles Scribner's Sons · New York

Copyright © 1976, 1972, 1969 Harry Milt

Library of Congress Cataloging in Publication Data

Milt, Harry.
   Alcoholism: Its Causes and Cure, A New
Handbook
   Published in 1969 under title: Basic handbook on
alcoholism.
   Bibliography: p. 143
   Includes index.
   1. Alcoholism. I. Title [DNLM: 1. Alcoholism—
Handbooks. WM274 M662n]
RC565.M54 1976   362.2'92   76–8476
ISBN 0–684–14667–3

Portions of this text appeared in *Basic
Handbook on Alcoholism*

Printed in the United States of America

1 3 5 7 9 11 13 15 17 19 H/C 20 18 16 14 12 10 8 6 4 2

To Jannie

Contents

Preface

In 1965, when the National Institute of Mental Health was considering the expansion of its sphere of interest to include alcoholism and other subjects that were then still peripheral to the Institute's central concern, the director of the Institute, Dr. Stanley Yolles, invited me to prepare monographs on the subjects under consideration. In preparing the monograph on alcoholism I realized that there was need for a book that would bring together a distillation of what was then known about the nature, origins, causes, development, and treatment of alcoholism, a book for both professionals and laymen. Thus was born the *Basic Handbook on Alcoholism,* the forerunner of the present volume.

The *Handbook* quickly became a standard auxiliary text in centers of alcohol studies, as well as in the curriculum of many universities, colleges, junior colleges, and schools of nursing. It also found wide public use through the National Council on Alcoholism and its affiliates and through community health centers and "crisis" clinics.

When I began work on revision of the *Handbook* in 1973, I was astounded at how many changes had taken place in the short time since its appearance. A great deal of new and exciting research had been produced, and a spirit of challenge to the established myths and dogmas was in the air. What was needed was not a mere revision but a complete new work. Material from the *Handbook* that is still useful has been retained, but it constitutes only a small part of *Alcoholism, Its Causes and Cure: A New Handbook.*

The present volume is intended to meet the needs both of professional people working with alcoholics, conducting research, or teaching and of people whose interest in alcoholism is of a personal nature. The objective has been to maintain scientific validity and maturity of thought while presenting the material in a way that would make it readily accessible to the lay public.

In the interest of readability, the text is unencumbered with reference notes. Works used in the preparation of the text are listed in the bibliography, which has been arranged by chapter. The most important works are identified in the text by author and sometimes by title as well so that the relevant work can be readily identified in the bibliography. Documentation is thus readily accessible to those who require it, without distracting the general reader with the mechanics of scholarship.

In his foreword to the *Handbook,* Mark Keller, editor of the *Journal of Studies on Alcohol,* called it "a clear display of the most important facts about alcoholism and a fair representation of the uncertainties." I have tried to maintain that standard.

Nearly all of the research for this book was done at the Rutgers University Center of Alcohol Studies, successor to the Yale Center of Alcohol Studies. There I had available its collection of books and journals, the Raymond G. McCarthy Collection of scholarly reprints, and the Classified Abstract Archive of the Alcohol Literature (CAAAL). I am grateful not only for the use of these materials but for the opportunities for consultation with the teachers and scholars at the Center, including the editors of the *Journal of Studies on Alcohol.*

I wish to acknowledge especially the cooperation of Timothy G. Coffey, managing editor of the *Journal,* who has over the years been a good friend and a source of continuing help, and that of Jane Armstrong, chief librarian at the Center.

ALCOHOLISM
Its Causes and Cure

A New Handbook

Introduction

Looking back over the history of alcohol studies, one is amazed to find that it is so short. It is, in fact, only a little more than thirty years old, having begun with the establishment in the early 1940s of the Yale Center of Alcohol Studies and the *Quarterly Journal of Studies on Alcohol.*

Those responsible for the stimulation of scientific interest in alcohol and alcoholism were motivated by humanitarian as well as academic concerns. Practically nothing was known, scientifically that is, about the action of alcohol on the body or about the medical, psychological, and behavioral consequences of drinking. Nor was anything known about the condition called alcoholism—its origins, causes, and development. There was only assumption, prejudice, and myth.

Scientific investigation would not only produce knowledge; it would also take alcoholism out of the realm of morality and bring it into the realm of medicine. If alcoholism could be established to be a sickness, it could no longer be regarded as a sin. This would relieve the alcoholic of unwarranted blame and reprobation. It would also win for him medical interest and the facilities for treatment and rehabilitation.

The effort to achieve for alcoholism accreditation as a disease was pursued through many channels, and the idea steadily won increasing public and professional acceptance. Finally, in 1956, the American Medical Association classified alcoholism as an illness.

In 1960 Dr. E. M. Jellinek, a leader in the movement and one of the founders of the Yale Center, produced *The Disease Concept of Alcoholism,* which sought, through a minute examination of the available scientific evidence together with some rather complicated hypothetical elaborations, to establish that alcoholism is not only a physical illness but also a physical addiction.

Dr. Jellinek also produced a "natural history" of alcoholism, outlining the phases and stages in the drinking history of an alcoholic. This formulation traced the typical development of alcoholism from its inception in casual drinking to culmination in total physical and psychological deterioration. It was republished several times during the author's lifetime with little modification.

Both these works sought to systematize existing knowledge about alcoholism and about the alcoholic and represented valuable contributions to the field. Unfortunately, however, despite the qualifications and cautions stressed by their author, the works have given rise to a rigid, deterministic concept of alcoholism which may be summarized as follows:

The alcoholic is born with a physiological or organic vulnerability to alcohol. When alcohol is consumed for some length of time, it triggers the unreeling of a well-defined, predetermined sequence of mental, physical, and behavioral reactions, moderate at first but becoming progressively worse. If this development is not interrupted by the abrupt and permanent cessation of drinking, it proceeds inevitably to total deterioration. If the development *is* interrupted by cessation, and then drinking begins again, the progression is resumed. In common parlance, "Once an alcoholic, always an alcoholic."

Dr. Jellinek also originated the concept of loss of control, distinguishing the alcohol addict from the nonaddicted drinker. A nonaddicted drinker can take a drink and stop. The addicted drinker is unable to stop and continues to drink until he falls unconscious or becomes too sick to drink any more. Loss of control is not present in the early stages of the development of alcoholism, because in these early stages dependence on alcohol is only psychological. Later on, physical dependence is superimposed on psychological dependence. A physiological change has taken place in the tissues—an alteration in cell metabolism—which produces an actual physical craving for alcohol. This physical craving causes the drinker to lose control—it compels him to keep on drinking once he has begun. This concept, too, has become solidly entrenched.

All these concepts and their underlying assumptions are now being questioned; some are being forthrightly challenged. Despite all efforts, no evidence has been produced to date of an inborn physiological or organic defect or aberration responsible for the development of alcoholism.

Furthermore, considerable doubt has been cast on the "inevitable progression" of the disease, and there are now some claims of spontaneous remission and some claims that the disease "burns itself out" after the age of 50. The once-an-alcoholic-always-an-alcoholic belief is being challenged by evidence purporting to show that some confirmed alcoholics have been cured of their disease and have been able to return to normal, social drinking.

There is evidence, also, that the chronic nature of alcoholism and its characteristic late-stage symptom picture are to some extent imposed by societal stereotypes and expectations to which the alcoholic passively conforms. Late-stage alcoholics taken out of the social milieu in which they have been drinking and placed in protected surroundings not only do not continue to drink obsessively but voluntarily stop. In laboratory situations they are quite able to limit their intake, starting and stopping when they wish and keeping their intake at very moderate levels in exchange for the reward of special privileges and comfortable living conditions.

The loss-of-control craving, or "once they start they can't stop" phenomenon, is controverted over and over again in laboratory situations by alcoholics who take a drink or two and then voluntarily stop. Many report that they do not even have the desire to drink.

Perhaps the most significant of these recent developments is the shift toward the belief that the underlying habituating or addictive process in alcoholism is psychological, not physical. This change in position is taking place not only with respect to alcohol but with respect to drug addiction as a whole. The World Health Organization's Expert Committee on Drug Dependence, composed of the world's leading authorities in pharmacology, regards all drug dependence—its term for drug addiction—to be primarily, if not entirely, a psychological phenomenon. This includes alcoholism. No credence whatever is given to the hypothesis of an alteration in cell metabolism or to any other hypothetical physiological or organic alteration out of which is presumed to grow a physical craving for alcohol.

In this perspective, the question of *cure* becomes quite pertinent. Those who hold that the disease itself is an inborn physical vulnerability of which uncontrollable drinking is just an expression insist there can be no cure. The drinking behavior may be brought to a permanent halt, but the disease itself cannot be cured.

On the other hand, many who regard the uncontrollable drinking itself to be the disease and who see no need to posit an inborn physical vulnerability consider the patient cured when the uncontrollable drinking has been brought to a halt for a considerable length of time. Since there is no underlying physical condition, there is nothing else to cure. When a cured alcoholic reverts to alcoholism after several years of abstention it means only that a learned response, once extinguished, has been reinstituted by a recurrence of internal psychological stress and external traumatic conditions similar to those which produced it in the first place. This behavior may be extinguished—cured—once more.

Thus the designation "cured" could be applied to those alcoholics who have gone back to normal social drinking, as well as to those who now abstain entirely.

1

How Alcohol Affects Behavior

Exploration of alcoholism begins with the agent itself.

Alcohol, also known as ethyl alcohol or ethanol, is a simple chemical. After it is swallowed, it passes into the stomach and then into the small intestine, where it is absorbed easily and quickly into the bloodstream and distributed to every part of the body. The disturbances of functioning known as intoxication are caused by the direct action of alcohol on the brain.

As the alcohol circulates through the body, enzymes act on it to metabolize it—to break it down into its simplest components, carbon dioxide and water. Most of this is done in the liver. Metabolism of alcohol takes place at a fairly constant rate. In a person weighing 150 pounds, the body breaks down about one-third of an ounce of alcohol in an hour. This is the amount contained in three-fourths of an ounce of 80- to 90-proof whiskey, gin, or vodka, in 2½ ounces of 12-percent table wine, or in 8 ounces of 4.5-percent beer. *amount of this is not*

Since only one-third of an ounce of alcohol is metabolized in an hour (in the 150-pound body) any quantity above that remains in the bloodstream, intact and active until it too is metabolized at the same rate. Thus, it would take two hours, roughly, to break down the alcohol in a 1½-ounce drink of straight whiskey, vodka, or gin, a 5-ounce glass of wine, or two 8-ounce glasses of beer.

Even in moderate social drinking, the rate of consumption is seldom limited to one drink of whiskey, one small glass of wine, or two glasses of beer during a two-hour period. Hence the alcohol accumulates more quickly than it is metabolized and the concentration of alcohol in the blood (the blood alcohol level) builds up. The higher the concentration of alcohol in the blood, the greater the concentration acting on the brain, and the greater the intoxication.

The speed with which a person becomes intoxicated depends on several factors:

Body Weight. The lighter the individual, the more slowly the alcohol is metabolized and the more quickly the blood-alcohol level builds up.

Speed of consumption. Gulping drinks one after another produces a high blood-alcohol level quickly; spacing of drinks moderates the effect.

Amount of food in the stomach. A full stomach passes its contents along to the small intestine much more slowly than an empty stomach. This accounts for the fact that a drink taken on an empty stomach is felt almost immediately; it is rushed to the small intestine, absorbed there into the bloodstream, and circulated to the brain in minutes. Conversely, a drink taken with or after a meal takes effect more slowly.

Concentration of alcohol. The higher the concentration of alcohol in the drink, the more rapidly it is absorbed. The alcohol in a straight drink is absorbed much more quickly than an equal amount of alcohol in a diluted drink or in wine or beer, even if consumed in the same amount of time.

Other chemicals in the drink. The greater the amount of nonalcoholic chemicals in the drink, the more slowly the alcohol is absorbed. For this reason, too, the alcohol in straight drinks, especially vodka and gin, is absorbed more rapidly than in mixed drinks, wine, or beer.

Nothing can reduce the blood-alcohol level except metabolism. "Sobering up" remedies have no effect whatever. Research has failed, to date, to produce a pharmacological agent that can speed up metabolism of alcohol. Once it is in the system, alcohol remains there to be metabolized bit by bit at the body's unhurried and unhurriable pace.

EFFECTS OF ALCOHOL

Alcohol produces its effects by depressing the functions of the central nervous system; other central nervous system depressants are morphine, heroin, and codein. They are distinguished from central nervous system stimulants, such as cocaine.

The pharmacological meaning of the term *depressant* should not be confused with the psychological use of that word. A psychological depressant is anything which produces the psychic state of depression characterized by intense dejection, deadening of feeling, unhappiness, lack of interest, spiritlessness, and hopelessness; a central nervous system depressant is very likely to act as a psychotropic antidepressant, relieving feelings of dejection and unhappiness and producing feelings of aliveness and pleasure.

Alteration of Moods and Emotions

As a psychic anesthetizer, alcohol provides relief from psychic distress including feelings of anxiety, depression, frustration, boredom, worry, and loneliness. It is also a euphoriant, producing feelings of pleasure, excitement, and well-being. It distorts the individual's perception of himself. When he is intoxicated, low self-esteem vanishes and he sees himself as attractive, important, successful, powerful, fearless, and confident: there is no problem he cannot solve, no obstacle he cannot overcome.

The moods that are produced are not always pleasant, however, nor do they necessarily remain so. Drinking may exacerbate an existing state of anxiety or depression, or a pleasant mood may give way to surliness, belligerence, and violence as drinking continues.

Drinking is also likely to bring into the open feelings of anger and hostility that have been lurking beneath the surface or to produce paranoid feelings of being misused, rejected, neglected, or victimized.

Disinhibition

Drinking relaxes inhibition and restraint. It makes it easier to take personal and social liberties. Cheating and stealing are no longer out of the question. Extramarital, premarital, and unconventional sex is engaged in without shame or guilt. Acts of daring, such as driving at a hundred miles an hour, "telling off the boss" and quitting a job, or "walking out on the family," may be committed without a second thought. In general, the disinhibiting effect of alcohol enables the drinker to do things he wanted to do while sober but could not do because of conscience, shame, guilt, fear, prudence, or common sense. Alcohol also derepresses impulses which have been repressed deeply out of consciousness, such as homosexual desires, incestuous desires, the urge to injure or kill, or the desire to abandon a child or mate.

Mental Processes

Alcohol distorts perception of time and space: events seem to be happening much more slowly than they actually are, and distances traveled are perceived as being much shorter than they are.

With the first drink or two an illusion may be created of clarity of mind and thought, and objects and ideas are perceived "as though through a crystal." As the alcohol continues to bathe the brain, however, consciousness becomes blurred, thinking is slowed down, the content of thought is impoverished, originality is reduced, ideas become stereotyped, memory is blurred, and there is considerable repetitiveness in conversation. Concepts are poorly formulated, reasoning is foggy, judgment is blunted.

Physical Effects

The first drink or two may have no observable physical effect; further intake definitely affects muscular coordination and control as well as balance, producing clumsy movements, slurred speech, stumbling, dropping or pushing over of objects, lurching, tripping, and difficulty in maintaining an upright position. Reaction time—the time elapsing between the receipt of a visual or auditory stimulus and the reaction to it—is slowed down. Sober, a driver may take no more than a tenth of a second to steer his car away from a child that has darted into the road; intoxicated, he may take a half a second or more, too long to avoid an accident.

ALCOHOL LEVEL IN THE BLOOD

Disturbances of functioning increase with the level of alcohol in the blood. To estimate the blood level or blood concentrations of alcohol, one needs such information as the amount and kind of beverage consumed in what space of time, the emptiness or fullness of the stomach, and the weight of the drinker. It is therefore impossible to generalize for all conditions, but it is possible to make a reasonably accurate estimate for a known set of conditions and to extrapolate from there.

A 150-pound drinker quickly consuming 90-proof whiskey on an empty stomach will have a peak blood alcohol level of 0.05 percent (0.05 grams per 100 cc of blood) with 3 ounces, 0.10 percent with 6 ounces, 0.15 percent with 9 ounces, 0.20 percent with 12 ounces, and 0.30 percent with 15 ounces. These figures would be slightly higher for gin or vodka or for a drinker weighing much less than 150 pounds. They would be somewhat lower for the equivalent amount of alcohol consumed in beer or wine, for drinking spaced over a period of time, for a drinker much heavier than 150 pounds, or for drinking accompanied by the eating of solid foods.

At 0.05 percent, the drinker is likely to feel the pleasant effects of moderate drinking—relaxation, relief from anxiety and tension, a sense of well-being, a "glow": inhibitions are relaxed, producing freer social interchange, conversation, and humor; problems are minimized or entirely forgotten. The mood change may, however, be in the opposite direction, manifested by irritability, testiness, anger, or belligerence.

At 0.08 percent, there is exaggerated and boisterous expression of the emotions with the beginning signs of unsteadiness, impairment of muscular coordination and control, and the slurring of speech.

Between 0.10 and 0.12 percent, intoxication is pronounced. There is definite impairment of muscular coordination, control, and balance. Objects are knocked over, the drinker stumbles and trips, thoughts become confused and uncertain; the drinker may become unguardedly amorous, insulting, or belligerent.

At 0.15 percent, intoxication is gross. Impairment of coordination and balance is extreme. The drinker staggers, stumbles, falls; or he may become so sleepy and stuporous that he will have to get off his feet.

At 0.20 percent, intoxication is extreme. The drinker will have lost control of his physical movements and balance completely and will be unable to move about without help. Emotions are out of control, and the drinker may thrash about, weep, or shout. Nothing he says will make any sense.

At 0.30 percent, he will be incapable of voluntary movement and be unaware of what he is seeing, hearing, or doing.

At 0.40 percent, he is in a coma. Any concentration beyond this will depress the brain center for respiration, breathing will stop, and the individual will die.

INDIVIDUAL DIFFERENCES IN REACTION

A phenomenon known as tolerance sets in after prolonged use of alcohol. When he first begins drinking, an individual may need only one drink to get "high." After a few years it may take two or three drinks to produce the same effect; after a decade, possibly four or five.

The reactions described for the different blood levels are those for a moderate drinker who has been drinking for a few years. For a person who has been drinking heavily for a long time, the reactions would be of lesser magnitude at each level than they would be for the average drinker. It is known, for example, that some alcoholics can consume a quart of whiskey or more a day without pronounced inebriation. They have also been known to perform complex tasks in the laboratory at blood alcohol levels much higher than those which would have produced severe behavioral disturbances in moderate-to-heavy drinkers.

There are also differences in reaction to alcohol within the individual. At one time, it may take four drinks to produce intoxication; at other times, two. On some occasions, alcohol may bring relief from anxiety; at other times it may have no effect at all or may even intensify psychic distress. Much depends on the individual's physical and emotional state at the time. Precisely what accounts for these differences is not yet known.

2

What Is Alcoholism?

People who drink do so for the effect, whether at a cocktail party, a luncheon, or a wedding, at home or at a bar. The effect they seek may be relaxation and pleasure, relief from depression or loneliness, or escape from unbearable pressures and problems.

 Alcohol also produces effects which are not desired. If too much alcohol is consumed, it causes the drinker to stagger, lose muscular control, think and speak incoherently, become boisterous and disorderly, and act rashly and with poor judgment. In greater quantities it may produce violence, acute physical illness, and loss of consciousness.

Most people who drink have no problem in stopping before the undesirable effects are produced. They have one or two drinks and stop, either because they simply do not have a desire for any more or because they begin to feel uncomfortable.

For many, however, there is a conflict. On one hand, there is the urge to keep on drinking in order to prolong the pleasure or relief; on the other there is the restraint of conscience, which says, "This is wrong," and of prudence, which says, "This is harmful." Generally, restraint prevails and the decision is made to halt.

This type of choice is made a hundred times a day in the ordinary course of living; not to have dessert because of the calories; not to buy an extra sweater or record because there are other priorities; not to chance a flirtation because of fidelity or fear of being found out. The desire for safety and the need to conform prevail over the impulse for immediate gratification or relief.

The opposite may also happen. The urge for immediate gratification or relief may be very powerful, and the restraining force very weak. In that event, control is overwhelmed, concern about the consequences are brushed aside, and the individual plunges ahead with whatever it is that is tempting him. This is the essence of compulsion.

The compulsive eater keeps on eating though it makes him ugly and increases his risk of illness and death. The compulsive smoker keeps on smoking though it may cause cancer. The compulsive drinker keeps on drinking though it may cost him his health, his job, and his family.

Compulsive drinking is the core symptom of alcoholism. Isolated, infrequent episodes of compulsive drinking do not constitute alcoholism. In alcoholism, as it is generally understood, compulsive drinking occurs repeatedly and frequently and continues to do so over a long stretch of time. It is generally described as addiction, although theories differ as to what addiction is (see chapter 7). The person is "hooked" on alcohol, he craves it, he must have it, he can't get along without it. Alcoholism can therefore be defined as a condition in which the individual drinks compulsively to the point of intoxication, does so repetitively, and continues to do so chronically.

This definition may be compared with others:

· In its 1967 *Report to the Nation,* the United States Cooperative Commission on the Study of Alcoholism defined alcoholism as "a condition in which individual has lost control over his alcohol intake in the sense that he is consistently unable to refrain from drinking or to stop drinking before getting intoxicated."

· The American Medical Association, in its *Manual on Alcoholism,* defines alcoholism as "an illness characterized by preoccupation with alcohol and loss of control over its consumption such as to lead usually to intoxication if drinking is begun; by chronicity; by progression; and by the tendency to relapse."

· Alcoholism is frequently referred to as alcohol addiction or alcohol dependence; both terms imply that the fundamental syndrome is a chronic and repetitive pattern of compulsive drinking. It may take many different forms, as illustrated by case histories:

Mrs. A., a middle-aged woman, had a combination of problems: alcoholism, inability to eat, and multiple food allergies. She rarely drank socially but drank alone several times a day —on arising, at lunch, and during the evening. Unless she drank on arising, she retched until exhausted. Unless she drank during lunch she was too anxious and tense to return to work. Without drinking she could not fall asleep.

Mrs. T., a nightclub entertainer, is a 35-year-old ambulatory schizophrenic who periodically becomes acutely anxious. Her drinking pattern is one of sporadic nipping at concealed liquor supplies. When her tension mounts to the point where it becomes acutely painful, she increases her tempo of drinking. When her anxiety becomes unbearable, she lapses into a temporary delusional psychosis which lasts from one to three days.

Ann began drinking at the age of 12. The first time she drank she became intoxicated. Following that experience she drank regularly on weekends. While babysitting for a neighbor, she and a group of friends would have a party and drink. Ann did not like beer, preferred whiskey, would drink anything. At the age of 13 she was committed to a training school for girls. Her later history was one of frequent drinking sprees and arrests.

Mr. L. is 38 years old, intelligent, a talented artist. He has been drinking on sporadic binges for twenty years. During the past eight years the binges increased markedly, necessitating a number of admissions to a state mental hospital. In his late drinking, nothing could stop him until he landed in the hospital. He is ridden with guilt of near psychotic proportions and believes that only when he is sick will the forces of evil leave him alone.

Irwin M., 53, illustrates the Skid Row pattern at the late stage of the career. Raised in the city streets, he quit school at the age of 16. His drinking began at the age of 20. He was first jailed for drunkenness at the age of 27 and since then has been committed 61 times for public intoxication. He is thoroughly addicted, drinks anything he can get, and can exercise no control once he starts drinking.

Richard R. is an advertising executive aged 52. He was brought to St. Vincent's Hospital in a state of near coma, having been discovered unconscious in the hotel room he had taken for a convention. He had begun to drink on the plane on the way to the meeting and continued to drink for four days until he collapsed. Episodes such as these had been occurring repeatedly for several years at functions away from home. Between these episodes, Mr. R. drinks normally and seldom becomes intoxicated.

Mr. C. was referred to an alcoholism clinic by the Circuit Court probation officer. He had been accused of molesting a minor female child while intoxicated. When sober he was meek and quiet; when intoxicated he was aggressive and antisocial. He had so many arrests for drunkenness that he lost count of them. Without exception, he drank until he passed out and was arrested.

Mr. Y. is a 50-year-old executive. Up to the age of 45 his alcohol intake had been moderate. Then his workload and responsibilities increased. To keep up with the pace he turned to alcohol. The extra drink at night helped him finish a particularly difficult job. Soon he began to need a drink in the afternoon, and then in the morning. Now he drinks day after day and remains in a continuous state of intoxication.

Although there is considerable variation in the patterns of drinking, there appear to be three predominant types. In *bout* drinking, the individual starts to drink and keeps on drinking hour after hour and day after day. When he stops, severe withdrawal reaction takes place. Recovery from the acute intoxication and withdrawal may take a few days to a few weeks. This is called the drying-out period. When it is over, there may be a few weeks of sobriety, followed by another bout, or a new bout may begin immediately after recovery from the last one.

The *daily* drinker drinks quite steadily hour after hour, and day after day, but not in increasing quantities and not to the point of severe intoxication. He spaces his drinking and limits the amount he drinks each time so as to maintain a constant state of moderate intoxication.

Periodic drinking is bout drinking which occurs on a regular weekly or monthly basis, or occurs only at times of great emotional stress, or in connection with special occasions where the restraints of home, family, and job are absent.

The range of case histories illustrates a fact well known to professionals but not quite so well known to the public: alcoholism is not confined to Skid Row. It is well distributed throughout all segments of society, including the well-to-do, the well educated, and the most highly respected.

Alcoholism may develop as early in life as the teens or as late in life as the sixties, but the onset is usually between 20 and 50. When it occurs early in life, it generally develops after a relatively short span of heavy drinking, some two to three years on the average. When it has its onset later in life, it generally takes much longer to develop, between six and ten years on the average.

Early alcoholism is generally associated with severe personality disorder, aggressive behavior, trouble with the police, difficulty in holding a job, and alienation from the family.

Those who become alcoholics early and in a short space of time are often referred to as *primary,* or *essential,* alcoholics, to indicate that their alcoholism stems from a basic character disorder. Those who become alcoholics later in life are referred to as *secondary,* or *reactive,* alcoholics, implying that they become dependent on alcohol as a result of severe emotional stress over a prolonged period, and not because of a basic character disorder.

Dr. Jellinek introduced a five-part Greek letter typology of alcoholism:

alpha alcoholics: excessive drinkers who do not lose control and who never become addicted.

beta alcoholics: drinkers whose symptoms are medical (as gastritis and cirrhosis of the liver) rather than behavioral or psychological.

gamma alcoholics: true alcohol addicts who lose control and drink in the bout pattern. This type is said to predominate in the United States.

delta alcoholics: true alcohol addicts whose style is daily drinking. Delta alcoholism is said to be the predominant type in wine-drinking countries such as France.

epsilon alcoholics: excessive drinkers formerly referred to as dipsomaniacs. Their style is the irregularly occasional bout. It bears some resemblance to the type others describe as periodic.

Nonprofessional organizations working with alcoholics commonly use the terms *gamma* and *delta* alcoholic, but this typology has found little acceptance professionally.

3

Alcoholism in Women

Alcoholism patterns are the same in women as in men. There are bout drinking, daily drinking, weekend binges, and irregular, occasional sprees. There are those who drink in nips and those who down copious quantities at a time. It begins in the same ways as it does in men and proceeds through similar stages, except that the speed of progression is usually faster for women than for men.

The two most common stereotypes of the woman alcoholic, that she is homosexual and that she is promiscuous, are not borne out by research. To the extent that these traits occur at all in alcoholism, they occur equally in both sexes.

There is no "typical" woman alcoholic, as the following case histories demonstrate:

Mary B., 43, has been an alcoholic from the time she was 20. Born into a second-generation welfare family, she has been dependent on some form of public assistance most of her life. She was married at 18 and was deserted after a few months. Since then she has been living for brief periods with one man after another. Her home has been in cheap furnished rooms or in shelters for homeless women. She is almost continuously drunk from inexpensive whiskey or wine purchased by means of welfare allowances or panhandling. She drinks alone, often in public parks.

Mrs. B.J., 40, is an editor. She took her first drink at the age of 26, when her fiancé left her. From then on she drank heavily every night and in a few months was drinking to oblivion. She developed paranoid tendencies believing that people were watching her and were aware of her drinking. After two or three years she controlled her drinking, found another man, and was married. With each emotional crisis, she plunges into a prolonged drinking bout.

Mrs. G.A., 34, is a model. She has been accustomed to alcohol since the age of 14 and began to drink excessively at 21. She goes on drinking binges lasting one or two weeks. She is subject to extreme mood swings and tantrums. When intoxicated, she runs around with strange men, showing no discrimination in her choice.

Miss V.H., 19, is a clerical worker. At a party given for her at age 14 she experienced severe emotional discomfort bordering on panic. Thereafter she refused all social invitations, until, at 17, a friend advised her to drink to ease her discomfort. She did, with the desired effect. From then on she drank not only before and during dates but in between. At 19 she sought treatment as an alcoholic.

Mrs. T.W., 52, is a housewife, married to a businessman, whom she discovered to be an alcoholic after their marriage. She herself seldom drank, and she became especially abstemious because of her husband's condition. At age 42, after an upsetting quarrel, she felt "heart pains" and called her doctor, who advised two shots of scotch. The remedy worked, and Mrs. W. continued to resort to it in other stressful situations. Her consumption increased, steadily growing into full-blown alcoholism.

Because society is much less tolerant of social deviance in women than in men, women alcoholics and their families conspire to maintain the image of innocence by hiding the problem from friends, relatives, and community. As a result, the woman alcoholic is hard to detect.

The great majority of women alcoholics drink at home and do not get into difficulty. It is only the small proportion who drink in public (bars, lounges, and parks) that become known to public agencies.

By and large, the "private" women alcoholics come from the lower-middle, middle, and upper classes. When they seek treatment, they do so through their own doctors or in private hospitals, private psychiatric centers, and community agencies serving the middle class. They are likely to be living with their families, working in business or a profession, and continuing to operate in the mainstream of "respectable" society.

The "public" female alcoholics tend to emerge from the lower socioeconomic strata. They are frequently in trouble with the police and seek or are brought to treatment in hospital emergency wards, in state mental hospitals, and in correctional institutions. They manifest a great deal of marital disruption and erratic work behavior and have in general made poor life adjustments. Their drinking and related problems begin earlier than those of other women alcoholics, and they show more problem behavior in childhood.

There is still no conclusive information on the proportion of female to male alcoholics. Studies based on population of alcoholics in such places as state mental hospitals and alcoholism clinics find that men alcoholics outnumber the women about five to one. In sharp contrast, private alcoholism treatment centers report a ratio of only three to one, and several private practitioners claim that among the thousands of patients they have seen over the years, the ratio is equal.

There is some evidence that the proportion differs with respect to socioeconomic status. Among the well-to-do there appear to be as many female as male alcoholics. Among the less privileged, the males outnumber the females four or five to one. This may mean that alcoholism is truly more prevalent among women of the upper socioeconomic brackets. Or it may mean that these women are more highly motivated to seek treatment, are better able to pay for it, and are therefore more likely to be counted than the others.

Male and female alcoholics also differ in their degree of social and psychological pathology. Women alcoholics are more frequently admitted to hospitals as psychiatric patients than as alcoholics, show a higher degree of mental illness, have more broken marriages, and make many more attempts at suicide.

The reasons women alcoholics give for drinking are largely concerned with female sex functions and family and love relationships, almost to the exclusion of all other reasons. The list includes premenstrual tensions, dysmenorrhea, menopause, hysterectomy, infertility, abortion, post-partum depression, miscarriage, frigidity, marital troubles, the demands of small children, boredom with household duties, loneliness and emptiness after the children are grown and gone, desertion, and divorce.

A striking number of the precipitating factors relate to the acceptance of femininity, and research confirms that a hidden conflict about femininity is typical of women alcoholics. As a rule, they are outwardly feminine in their behavior and see themselves as being decidedly womanly, but tests indicate that they unconsciously identify with the masculine sex role. There are also indications that, in spite of their strong motivation to be "womanly," "good mothers," and "good wives," women alcoholics are unconsciously quite insecure in these roles, doubting their adequacy as women. They are constantly accepting traditionally feminine roles and claim to receive gratification from them, yet underneath they are extremely anxious about their performance and about their ability to live up to the expectations of their husbands and of society.

There is also among women alcoholics a pattern of poor self-image, feelings of inadequacy, fear of loneliness and isolation, and excessive needs for affection, love, and attention. They react much more intensely to the loss of a loved one than do male alcoholics.

4

Development of Alcoholism

No two cases of alcoholism develop in exactly the same way. Yet those who have studied alcoholics at close range agree that it is possible to delineate a course of development which would fit, in its broad outlines, a large proportion of the alcoholics who come in contact with alcoholism treatment centers, alcoholism clinics, private physicians and psychiatrists, and Alcoholics Anonymous.

The progression is marked off into stages, each with its own mental, emotional, and behavioral characteristics. While the following account carries the progression to its ultimate stages, it must be recognized that not all cases are so severe or so extreme. Many are interrupted by treatment or by circumstances which alter their course, and some alcoholics, it now appears, even recover from alcoholism spontaneously (see chapter 11).

INITIATION

All drinking starts in a social setting, such as the home, the school, the club, a gathering of friends, a celebration, or a party. For some, the new experience does nothing at all and is not likely to be repeated unless the occasion calls for it. Others find that drinking relaxes them, makes them feel good, gives them a glow, or temporarily eases a worry or a disappointment. For a few, the effect is dramatic. Many alcoholics describe their first drinks with such phrases as: "like magic," "made me feel wonderful," "like being born all over again," "my whole life had changed," "felt better than I had ever felt before." With just a drink or two, they recollect, it was possible to feel attractive, brilliant, important, witty, powerful.

Those for whom alcohol renders such wonderful changes are the ones most likely to become alcoholics. Until their encounter with alcohol, they have had to bear their dejection, anxiety, boredom, shyness, and feelings of inferiority without relief. Alcohol has now provided them with a miraculous remedy.

There is no indication that the potential alcoholic makes a conscious connection between the drinking and the relief it brings. He senses only that the drinking provides a pleasurable experience which he would like to enjoy again. Hence he begins to seek out situations in which drinking is expected to take place, such as a party, a luncheon, a stopover at a bar with friends on the way home. These are casual, normal drinking situations and become easily integrated into the regular routine of life without arousing notice.

INCREASE IN INTAKE

After a year or two, or possibly more, a change becomes noticeable. The alcoholic-to-be not only seeks out occasions for drinking, he now begins to invent them. Friends are invited over to watch TV or play cards, and drinks are served. Neighbors are invited to drop in for a drink after dinner, or on weekends. Along with the increase in the occasions for drinking there is a steady increase in the amount consumed: the cocktail before lunch or dinner becomes two, the "quick one" on the way home becomes two or three, and the nightcap becomes a prolonged drinking session.

DEVELOPMENT OF DEPENDENCE

Next, a new and telling change takes place. Drinking and drinking occasions begin to lose their lighthearted, spontaneous tone. From being a way of having fun and enjoying life they become a dead serious business. The pattern has become compulsive.

If a drinking routine has been set, it may not be altered. The cocktail hour before dinner becomes a sacred ritual with which nothing may interfere. The family may wish to have an early dinner because of something they wish to do later, but this will not do. If, on a theater night, the regular two cocktails before dinner may mean missing the curtain, "then we will just have to be late." If the couple is going to a party, the alcoholic-to-be "has a few" before leaving home. When he arrives at the party and the host is slow in serving the drinks, he offers to help out.

Drinks which used to be sipped are now gulped, as though to hasten the effect, and it now takes two or three drinks to produce the effect that one used to have, evidence that the body is developing a tolerance for alcohol. Drinking has become a daily practice, most of it being done in the evening. Consumption is heavy but not yet conspicuous, and intoxication is subdued.

As drinking increases in frequency and volume, there is a noticeable change in the drinker's personality. He becomes easily and frequently irritated, edgy, nervous, and depressed. Things bother him which did not bother him before. There are frequent headaches, nights of insomnia, tiredness, stretches of feeling "just plain rotten." A chip-on-the-shoulder attitude becomes evident, with a tendency to hear criticisms where none were expressed or intended and a trigger-readiness to snap back at the imagined offender. There are outbursts of jealous anger without cause. Frequent lightning changes in mood take place, a Jekyll-Hyde alternation between friendliness and antagonism. Above all, there is hypersensitivity about discussion of the drinking; any mention of it is likely to bring on an explosion.

The existence of a drinking problem is denied and the heavy drinking is rationalized by a variety of excuses: he drinks no more than most of his friends; he drinks because he enjoys it and is entitled to his own form of pleasure; he drinks because he has so many things to worry about; he has to drink because he has been feeling sick.]

As his personality difficulties bring him into conflict with—and consequently isolation from—those around him, [there emerges a complex of self-centeredness, selfishness, and grandioseness. The incipient alcoholic appears to become a world unto himself. His conversations become monologues, uninterrupted recitations about his aspirations, worries, conquests, problems, frustrations. His needs, not only for alcohol but for comforts and luxuries, must be satisfied before those of others, including his children and wife, and they must be satisfied immediately. He is convinced, and eagerly attempts to convince others, that he is on the verge of great success, that he is being sought out for the managership of his firm, that he has worked out a system to beat the market. Needless to say, his grandiose elaborations are without substance, and when they are acted on as though they are real, they are likely to end in disaster. This phase may last for three or four years.

ADDICTION, EARLY PHASE

Then two new and frightening symptoms appear—the blackout and the first drinking bout.

The Blackout

On the day after a heavy drinking episode, the individual is asked about something that had happened in the midst of the drinking, and he is unable to remember it, even vaguely. It is as though a segment of time had been erased completely from his memory, even though the period in question had not been marked by extreme intoxication. Infrequent at first, blackouts begin to occur quite regularly.

The Bout

Drinking has been steady and heavy but it has been restricted mainly to evening hours, starting earlier only on weekends. Then one day—generally on a weekend—the first bout begins. Having started to drink, the individual has one drink after another, becoming more and more intoxicated until, late in the evening or early in the morning, he falls into a stuporous sleep. The following morning he begins to drink almost immediately on awakening and continues to do so throughout the day, and again on the following day.

The first bout may last only two or three days, terminating when the individual has to return to work, and there may not be another one for weeks or months. Eventually, however, the weekend bout becomes an almost regular occurrence and the "weekends" stretch into Monday and Tuesday.

Then comes the time when the bouts turn into benders, when the drinking continues day after day, for a week or two or three, until the body rebels and the drinker becomes so sick that he simply cannot consume any more.

Withdrawal Symptoms

With the cessation of drinking the individual experiences withdrawal symptoms, ranging from tremulousness through hallucinosis, convulsions, and in the most extreme form, delirium tremens (DTs).

Tremulousness, the least extreme form, is manifested by "shakes," jitters, restlessness, agitation, nausea, loss of appetite, insomnia, nightmares when sleep does occur, muscular weakness, depression and anxiety, and the craving for alcohol or a sedative to ease the acute discomfort.

Hallucinosis may occur along with tremulousness and its accompanying symptoms. The drinker thinks he hears voices accusing, insulting, or threatening him. He may also imagine he sees or smells things which are not there.

A few alcoholics also have "rum fits," convulsions similar to those in epilepsy. Some physicians regard this condition as evidence of an underlying epileptic constitution. Alcoholics who have rum fits are the ones who are likely to experience delirium tremens later in their drinking careers.

Delirium tremens occurs in a small proportion of cases after prolonged benders lasting five or six weeks or more. The alcoholic undergoes terrifying visual and auditory hallucinations. He is completely disoriented and severely agitated. He may be so frightened by his hallucinations and delusions that he may harm himself or others.

Realization

Between bouts the alcoholic may strive heroically to free himself of his addiction. He may abstain from alcohol for weeks, or change the time and place of his drinking, the occasions for drinking, and the kind of liquor he drinks.

None of these changes makes any difference, and he finally abandons himself to the realization that he has indeed become an alcoholic and that liquor is vital to his existence. He believes he cannot exist without it and proceeds to "protect his supply," keeping a good quantity always at hand and hiding it so his resentful family will not destroy it.

ADDICTION, LATE PHASE

Now a new symptom appears, morning drinking.

Regular drinking continues between bouts, but the evening's drinking does not "sleep itself off" as before. Now the morning hangover is so severe that a drink must be had immediately on waking. An hour or two later, another drink is needed, and then another an hour or two after that.

Gradually the gap between morning drinking and afternoon

drinking is closed, and drinking is continuous. The bouts, which have been widely spaced, come closer and closer together until one follows immediately on recovery from the last.

Alcohol now dominates the alcoholic's entire life. He has been abandoned by his family and has lost his job, his friends, and his connection with normal society. He will drink with anyone and will drink anything he can get his hands on. His thinking is drastically impaired, as is his sense of ethical behavior.

Two types of alcoholic psychoses are likely to occur, Wernicke's syndrome and Korsakoff's syndrome, both marked by confusion, wandering of the mind, stupor, and loss of memory.

Serious physical illness is brought on by saturation with alcohol, deterioration of nutrition, and exposure to the elements. At this advanced stage, the alcoholic is subject to cardiac strain, gastritis, hemorrhage of the esophagus, liver damage, emphysema, diabetes, and pneumonia.

Death from any of these causes or from suicide is not uncommon.

5

Effect on Family Life

Families react to the problem of alcoholism in more or less the same way. It is possible, on the basis of several studies, to outline a typical sequence of events, including those which follow recovery.

EMERGENCE OF THE PROBLEM

At the time of marriage the man's drinking is, in most cases, still within accepted bounds. Men who are already alcoholics manage to hide the fact from their fiancées. The first occurrence of a drinking problem comes, therefore, as a surprise. It generally takes place at a social function and is manifested as offensive drunkenness, disturbing boisterousness, or an unprovoked, noisy quarrel.

After several such episodes the wife becomes upset and angry and confronts the husband. He either concocts some acceptable explanation and promises it will not happen again or refuses to discuss the matter. The incident is not repeated for a while and the problem is forgotten.

Then another incident occurs, and the process repeats itself.

Having no notion that she is witnessing the signs of early alcoholism, the wife deals with the problem drinking as she might with any other kind of troublesome behavior: she scolds and brings on a quarrel; she ignores the problem, hoping it will go away by itself; she discusses it with friends and relatives who either reassure her and advise her not to worry or advise her to "give him a good talking to."

Occasionally excessive drinking occurs at home, but the problem does not yet occur with sufficient frequency or gravity to provoke a family crisis. The wife still does not see it as a special problem—certainly not as alcoholism—and expects that ultimately reason, persuasion, threats, or "time" will take care of it. Between episodes tension and anxiety are reduced, and life continues much as usual.

INTENSIFICATION OF
THE PROBLEM

As the months go by, the episodes become more frequent and disturbing. Friends react by excluding the couple from social activities and friendship groups. The wife, with awareness of the problem thus thrust upon her, turns down some of the invitations that do come and gives up having gatherings in her own home.

The isolation throws the family members into closer contact with each other, intensifying and magnifying the drinking problem which is now showing up in drunkenness, quarreling, destructiveness, and abusiveness at home.

The fear of discovery haunts the wife and she does her best to cover it up with explanations of sickness to her children, relatives, the employer. She does not yet consider seeking help from social agencies or, in case of violence, from the police, for fear of degrading and stigmatizing her family.

The conflict between wife and husband becomes intense and they draw farther apart. Increased tension produces increased drinking, which produces increased tension. In an effort to escape from this unbearable situation husband and wife may have a period of "sweet reasonableness" in which they join forces to explore the reasons for the drinking, hoping that if they can discover the reason they can solve the problem. This is inevitably unproductive and is followed by anger and recrimination.

The husband plunges more deeply into his own sense of isolation, helplessness, and desperation—and is thrown more than ever on his only resource, alcohol. The wife begins to blame herself. Each failure to help her husband eats away at her own sense of adequacy, as a wife and as a person.

In the desperate struggle to maintain a hold on his life and to escape from the obsession with alcohol, the husband manages periods of sobriety. Each such period brings a new burst of hope. The husband is convinced he has finally mastered the problem. He is contrite, remorseful, thankful for his wife's forgiveness. The wife, feeling a tremendous sense of relief and thinking the problem at an end, regains her affection and concern for her husband and her own sense of adequacy and worthiness. But the inevitable relapse occurs, and the family is thrown once again into bewilderment, conflict, and despair.

Even at this stage, when the husband's inability to control his drinking is so painfully obvious, neither he nor his wife can recognize and acknowledge that he is an alcoholic. The psychological mechanism of denial protects them from the terror and shame which recognition and acknowledgment would bring. The condition continues to be regarded as a "drinking problem," but the wife has exhausted her resources to deal with the problem rationally. All her efforts are bent on keeping her husband from drinking. Now begins the frantic hiding or emptying of bottles, efforts to cut off the husband's supply of money, and the canceling of charge accounts—or, on the other hand, the cajoling, pampering, and placating of the husband, even to the extent of drinking with him.

While this is going on there is still an effort to keep the family functioning as a family. In periods of sobriety the husband is still deferred to as head of the household, and the children are still expected to respond to him with respect and obedience. But it is impossible to maintain even this shaky equilibrium; the conflict, anger, fear, and resentment are too intense.

DISINTEGRATION OF
FAMILY LIFE

The children are brutally buffeted as they struggle to maintain their sanity, sense of security, and identity in the mounting turmoil. Sooner or later, the inevitable consequences are manifested: emotional disturbances, psychosomatic illness and, if the children are old enough, "acting out"—sexual promiscuity, running away from home, failures in school work, stealing.

Having failed in all her efforts to restore her husband to sobriety, the wife throws up her hands and recognizes that the problem is beyond her.

At this point, open warfare may break out, with resort to violence on both sides. The wife alternates between terror of her husband and unrestrained belligerence. When her anger is spent, she feels loathing for what she has become. Sex has long since waned to sporadic occurrences and now disappears altogether, as she withdraws from any affectionate contact with her husband, emotional or physical.

By this time, also, the husband's drinking has produced difficulty with the police and the inevitable nights in jail. Now all is chaos. Life consists of one impossible situation after another—drunkenness, violence, quarreling, fighting, arrests, outbreaks of illness, and problem behavior of the children.

Seeing that it is impossible for things to continue this way much longer and that some radical change must take place, the wife may leave or force the husband to leave, but in most cases, there is an intervening stage before the rupture takes place. This is the stage in which the wife pushes the husband aside and takes over the direction and leadership of the family.

EMERGENCE OF A NEW FAMILY PATTERN

One after another, the father's roles and prerogatives are taken away from him. The wife becomes the manager, the disciplinarian, the decision maker. If the husband is still working, she finds a way to get control of his paycheck and doles out his allowance. When he drinks, she may refuse to feed or take care of him and may lock him out of the house. Following their mother's lead, the children are critical of him, talk back to him, and treat him like a misbehaving child.

The father feels completely defeated, and his drinking bouts become longer and more frequent. By this time, he has very likely lost his job and has found himself in the hospital several times for acute intoxication and withdrawal and for one or more of the severe illnesses common to alcoholics (pneumonia, gastritis, liver disorders, malnutrition). The husband's alcoholism is now known to all, and the wife no longer hesitates to call upon outside help—family agencies, Alcoholics Anonymous, the police, family court.

Through these outside contacts she becomes aware of alcoholism as an illness. She gains insight into her husband's problems and the possibilities for control and rehabilitation through Alcoholics Anonymous, clinics, and other agencies in the community. She regains her own confidence and self-esteem and in the process gains a sense of her own importance and capabilities as an individual entirely apart from her role as wife and mother.

With the family completely reorganized around the mother, one of two things may happen: she may leave her husband (or find a way to force him out), or he may undertake treatment and start on the road to rehabilitation.

When Wife and Husband Separate

If the wife decides that her only recourse is to break with her husband, she must still contend with many psychological and practical difficulties. While she feels completely justified in the separation and knows that it will be best for herself and the family, she may continue to feel great concern and responsibility for the husband, who is now entirely alone, sick, and virtually helpless. She may also be concerned with what the relatives will say about "abandoning her husband in his hour of need."

Further, she is worried about being able to work and earn enough to support the family, about the prospect of loneliness, the loss of security, and fright at embarking on a style of life that is utterly new and strange to her.

She has also to deal with her husband's threats to do harm to her, the children, or himself should she leave him.

On the other hand, she knows that if she cannot help her husband, she can and must help herself and her children. Besides, her confidence has been strengthened by her ability to reorganize the family and take over its management; by this time, she has very likely found work and made some arrangements for the care of the children.

Finally, the decision is made. She begins proceedings for separation and divorce and starts a new life without her alcoholic husband. She is, in most cases, not yet free of him, for he will continue to attempt to come back into the family, try to talk to her at her place of employment, threaten her and the children with violence, or appeal to the children to persuade their mother to have him come back. These efforts usually fade, however, and the family begins its new life.

When the Husband Goes for Treatment and Recovers

If the alcoholic receives treatment and recovers, the family's problems are still not over. First, there is the problem of the restructured family. The mother is now in full control and comfortable in her new role, and the children are oriented around her leadership. It is difficult for mother and children to forget the suffering of the past several years or to efface the mistrust, resentment, and hostility that has developed. Unsure of the permanence of the father's recovery, they remain in a constant state of anxiety.

The recovered alcoholic knows that he has lost stature and is eager to regain it. More often than not, he moves aggressively and insistently, arousing resentment and conflict. He fears and resents his family's mistrust.

Another major problem is the unrealistic expectation that with the elimination of the drinking a blissful family life will ensue. This attitude overlooks the interpersonal conflicts, the problems other than drinking, which might in fact have contributed to the drinking. These other problems may include immaturity, insecurity, selfishness, efforts of one to control the other, excessive demand for affection and devotedness, neurotic anxieties and compulsions, and all the other aberrations which often lead to separation and divorce.

Unless these problems are handled, and it is practically impossible to handle them without the help of outside agencies (such as family agencies, psychotherapy, Alcoholics Anonymous, or Al-Anon, an organization of relatives and friends of alcoholics), there is little hope that the recovered alcoholic can maintain his sobriety.

EFFECT ON THE CHILDREN

Alcoholism in the family is especially difficult for the children and leaves them with psychological injuries they will bear the rest of their lives. It is axiomatic that for good mental health a child needs to feel adequate and worthwhile, to have a sense of trust in others, to have confidence in his ability to handle the challenges of growing up. These feelings are engendered by a climate of safety and certainty in the home, by unwavering warmth and affection from the parents, by orderliness and certainty in the surroundings, and by consistent control and discipline from mother and father, none of which is likely to be found in a home shaken by alcoholism.

Upset by her husband's alcoholism and by her own travail, the mother is unable to provide the warmth, protection, and affection the children need. Instead she is frequently depressed, distraught, angry, and punitive.

The father, instead of providing the children with a model of manliness, direction, and mastery over his surroundings, presents a picture of helplessness, confusion, and abject cringing when he is sober and of abandon, wanton irresponsibility, cruelty, and abuse when he is drunk.

The parents lean on the children emotionally and attempt to undermine each other's position in the children's affections. The children are torn by feelings of disloyalty and guilt and by fears of punishment and rejection.

When the mother is the alcoholic, she is even less capable of providing the children with the necessary emotional nurture.

Instead of being able to develop their personalities by identifying with parents they admire, the children are left with a confused sense of their own identity and a diffuse self-image. For the rest of their lives they have difficulty in defining themselves in adult roles as parents, mates, homemakers, and breadwinners. Self-esteem is damaged by the stigma of having an alcoholic parent who is often in trouble with the law and by avoidance and ostracism from their friends.

The children of troubled families often see themselves as the cause of the families' difficulties and invite punishment by "acting out"; or they punish themselves with neurotic reactions, psychosomatic illnesses, or even psychoses. Prolonged immersion of a child in a family with alcoholism is also likely to create the emotional conditions for which the child will in turn seek relief from alcohol: anxiety, depression, low self-esteem, poor impulse control, low tolerance for emotional pain, and the need for immediate relief.

6

The Roots of Alcoholism

Those who regard alcoholism as a disorder arising from psychological causes formulate their hypothesis as follows: People who become alcoholics are psychologically alcoholism-prone, predisposed by two basic conditions. One is an unremitting burden of emotional distress made up of anxiety, depression, repressed anger, aloneness, and low self-esteem. The other is a cluster of personality traits which limit the individual's capacity to deal realistically with emotional problems and the problems of living—low tolerance for frustration and suffering, the need for immediate gratification, poor impulse control, and low coping capability or "ego strength." This person has an urgent need for (1) relief from his emotional distress; (2) an easy source of gratification, pleasure, and self-esteem; and (3) a way to deal with the reality he cannot handle. Alcohol provides all of these. It anesthetizes emotional pain, produces euphoria, aggrandizes the ego, and modifies reality so the drinker does not have to deal with it. Dependency on alcohol for these effects is at first limited, but it expands, crowding out realistic alternatives until, eventually, it dominates the personality completely.

The evidence for the psychological view and for the physical view will be explored in this and the following chapter.

EVIDENCE FOR THE
PSYCHOLOGICAL VIEW

In a nationwide survey of treatment methods and facilities, more than 150 professionals treating alcoholics were asked to identify the core personality characteristics of their patients. Reporting on the results in his *Treatment of Alcoholics,* Sidney Cahn related that the traits most consistently mentioned were anxiety, depression, self-depreciation, dependency, compulsiveness, and immaturity.

Similarly, Dr. Eva M. Blum and Dr. Richard H. Blum, in *Alcoholism: Modern Psychological Approaches to Treatment,* identify the personality traits most commonly mentioned in relation to alcoholics as anger, restlessness, depression, insecurity, conflict, anxiety, deep guilt, lack of self-esteem and self-assertion, emotional instability, low frustration tolerance, and high but unfulfilled aspirations.

Alcoholics themselves attest to the fact that these traits were present before drinking began and that they turned to drinking because of them. Confirmation comes also from more objective sources.

Dr. Mary C. Jones, a psychologist, did a follow-up study, covering thirty years, of several hundred children who had been brought up in Oakland, California. Since greatly detailed information was available about the subjects in their childhood, it was possible to single out characteristics peculiar to those who had become alcoholics. The research disclosed that these individuals had indifferent, rejecting mothers and lived in families that lacked warmth and understanding. From early childhood on, these individuals had more tensions, fewer satisfactions, and fewer ways of handling their difficulties.

Similar findings were reported by Dr. Joan McCord and Dr. William McCord, sociologists, working from greatly detailed data on several hundred boys who had been observed originally in the Cambridge-Somerville (Mass.) Youth Study in the 1930s and whose progress was recorded as they grew up.

The McCords found considerable evidence of family instability, absence of maternal warmth and support, poorly defined parental control, mothers' resentment of their maternal role, fathers' evasion of their role as males, and failure of both parents to set up role expectations for their sons—conditions leading quite understandably to anxiety, depression, insecurity, poor impulse control, and low self-esteem.

Many other significant factors have been disclosed about the childhood experiences and conditions of alcoholics. Broken homes and loss of one or both parents through death or other causes are a common finding, as is a high degree of antisocial behavior on the part of parents, brothers, and sisters. Alcoholism in one or both parents is found very frequently. There is almost always great discord between the parents, with one being in a dominant, aggressive position and the other in a passive, submissive position.

Summarizing the research findings, it can be said that, as a result of trauma experienced in childhood, people who become alcoholics grow up with a great deal of insecurity, tension, anxiety, and conflict; that many turn to alcohol quite early in their youth to assuage these feelings; and that they continue to do so throughout adult life.

DEPENDENCY AND DEPENDENCY CONFLICT

A great deal has been said about dependency conflict as a special factor predisposing the individual to alcoholism. Dependency in this context has little to do with the dependence of one person on another for having things done for him; it has rather to do with the dependence for love, affection, protection, and indulgence. All children require care; a dependent child is one who needs steady demonstration of love and admiration from the mother or father. Such dependency is the normal state in infancy and early childhood. As the child grows, he is weaned away from so close and needy a relationship, differentiates himself as a separate individual, and draws satisfaction from his own activity, assertiveness, and achievement.

A child whose normal movement away from dependency is

impeded continues to yearn for close ties to his mother. However, he dares not express it. If he expresses it, he runs counter to society's expectations of him. Achievement, independence, self-reliance, power, drive, and assertiveness are socially valued. Sentimentality, submissiveness, softness, and dependency are frowned upon.

The child is therefore in constant conflict. He wants to feel submissive and dependent, but dares not. These feelings are repressed, and they persist into adult life on an unconscious level, creating continuous, unexplainable anxiety. When a young man with this problem encounters alcohol, he has found "the perfect solution." Not only does alcohol relieve anxiety; it also resolves his conflict. Under the influence of large doses of alcohol he can feel comforted, cared for, and safe (dependent). He can also be "masculine," assertive, and aggressive (nondependent).

The McCords' study was one of the most extensive research investigations of this subject. It was their belief that the most intense dependency conflict is created by mothers who alternate between lavish indulgence of a child's dependency needs and punishment for the very same desires. The study bore out their hypothesis. They found that the mothers who alternated between affection and rejection produced the highest proportion of alcoholic sons, more, even, than did mothers who rejected their children outright.

The McCords were convinced from these findings and from observations in other studies they had made that "anxiety generated by an intense dependency conflict produces alcoholism."

There is other evidence that dependency conflict exists in the childhood of alcoholics. As a rule, male alcoholics are recalled as having been aggressive, assertive, and independent as boys. Psychological tests of overt behavior and feelings confirm these impressions, but psychological tests of unconscious feelings reveal softness, passivity, and nonmasculine dependency.

THE PSYCHOANALYTIC EXPLANATION

The psychoanalytic explanation of the origins of alcoholism concerns itself primarily with the disturbances in the development of the personality in infancy and childhood. The infant is said to pass through several clearly defined stages, each characterized by increasingly mature levels of self-sufficiency, independence, control of behavior, mastery of surroundings, and healthy relatedness to others, including friendship and heterosexual love.

If the child is unable to make successful transition from one stage to the next, his personality becomes fixated there and for the rest of his life he will manifest the immature personality characteristics of that stage. Some people who do move up the ladder of personality development do so on a tenuous basis. When subjected to stress, they regress to an infantile level. Alcoholism is believed to result from fixation at or regression to one of these early stages of personality development.

Oral Stage

At the oral stage there is undifferentiated need for and expression of love (for and from everybody). There is also narcissistic self-love, clinging to mothering persons, and depressive moods when love support is not forthcoming. There is intolerance of frustration, pain, and anxiety, and there is irresponsibility and emotional instability. Impulsiveness and need of immediate gratification are also present. Most of these traits are found, characteristically, among the so-called primary or essential alcoholics.

Anal Stage

At the anal (sphincter control) stage of personality development the child is beginning to assert selfhood. Persons arrested at this stage manifest aggressiveness, cruelty, obstinacy, and rebelliousness, all related to the sense of being a distinct person and desire to preserve the emerging identity. They also manifest a drive for mastery and achievement, related to the acts of walking, talking, and muscular coordination. A more advanced defense mechanism, sublimation, is available at this stage. Hence, an anally fixated alcoholic is able to divert his energy from drinking to more useful kinds of behavior. He is active rather than passive and manipulates his environment; therefore, his prognosis is better.

Love relationships at the anal stage are no longer undifferentiated or self directed; they are directed to others, but not necessarily of the opposite sex. Alcoholics fixated at this level are likely to have homosexual desires which have been either sublimated into friendships with members of the same sex or repressed entirely. Since alcohol "dissolves" sublimations and repressions, homosexual tendencies may emerge in undisguised form when the alcoholic is intoxicated.

Phallic-Oedipal Stage

Individuals fixated at the phallic-oedipal level have progressed beyond homosexual love but have not yet emerged from oedipal attachment to the mother. As adults their life is complicated by their inability to cope with authority figures (father substitutes) or to direct themselves in frank sexuality to members of the other sex. This type of personality tends toward friendliness, affability, and formation of superficial relationships. The surface friendliness hides barely repressed anger, rebelliousness, fear of sexual inadequacy, low self-esteem, and compensatory overactivity and competitiveness. These characteristics are found in many alcoholics.

Individuals arrested at an early stage of development will continue to behave in an infantile and immature way. The earlier the level of fixation, the more severe will be the drinking problem and the less hopeful the prognosis. Individuals who have achieved emotional maturity but who have regressed under the stress of unfavorable life circumstances have a much better outlook for recovery.

Alcoholism and Psychiatric Illness

Since alcoholism may be the result of fixation at one of several different stages of development, it is often associated with the other personality disturbances which result from fixation at that stage. Persons with character disorders or schizophrenia, for example, are believed to be fixated at the earliest stage, the oral. Persons with psychoneuroses are believed to be either fixated or regressed to the anal or oedipal level.

One of the earliest pieces of research on this subject was conducted by an American psychiatrist, Dr. Mary Jane Sherfey, at the Payne Whitney Clinic in New York. Studying the records of hundreds of alcoholic patients, Dr. Sherfey found that they fell into two groups. Half were in a category in which alcoholism was another symptom in a well-defined psychopathology. The diagnoses in this group were paranoid schizophrenia, manic-depressive psychosis, psychopathic personality, psychoneurotic personality, epilepsy, and brain damage. The other patients had been admitted with the primary diagnosis of alcoholism, but when they were more closely scrutinized they were found to be suffering from such disorders as rigidly organized neurotic personalities with paranoid features; dependent psychoneurotic personalities with depression and tension; middle- and late-life depressions. "In none of these cases," Dr. Sherfey observed, "did alcoholism exist without previous personality defects antedating drinking. . . . This is not to say that there may not be alcoholics who have no demonstrable defects serious enough to be termed illness. In our experiences, however, they must be rare."

Subsequently, dozens of other studies were made on the relationship between alcoholism and psychiatric disorder. They confirm Dr. Sherfey's finding that alcoholism is invariably found in association with psychiatric illness. The specific disorders which have shown up most frequently in cases of alcoholism are neurosis, passive aggressive personality, compulsive personality, schizoid personality, paranoid personality, borderline schizophrenia, schizophrenia, psychotic depressive reaction, and manic-depressive psychosis. These studies are summarized by Dr. Herbert

Barry III in his *Psychological Factors in Alcoholism*.

Alcoholism is also known to be an important factor in suicides. One study after another has shown that between 25 and 35 percent of all suicides have a definite history of alcoholism. This is not surprising, since many of the personality characteristics, psychiatric illnesses, and childhood antecedents found in alcoholism are also found in suicide.

The Alcoholic Personality

The foregoing discussion should dispel any notion that there is a special type of alcoholic personality. Many research investigations have been initiated to see whether such an entity does indeed exist, and all conclude that it does not. Alcoholism and the cluster of personality traits which predispose an individual to it are found in a wide variety of personality structures, all of which have just one thing in common, psychiatric disorder.

PHYSICAL EXPLANATIONS

Opposing the view that alcoholism is caused psychologically is the belief that the alcoholic is born with a physiological or organic defect responsible for the craving for alcohol or for an inability to control the impulse to drink.

Nutritional Theory

The nutritional theory of alcoholism rests on the premise of a metabolic defect which results in a bodily requirement for the intake of alcohol. The first research attempting to substantiate this belief was conducted by the physiologist Dr. Jorge R. Mardones and his colleagues at the University of Chile in the 1940s. In a series of experiments they demonstrated that when rats were deprived of Vitamin B complex and offered a choice between water and alcohol solution, they preferred the alcohol. From this Dr. Mardones reasoned that the alcoholic's craving for alcohol results from an inborn nutritional defect similar to the one induced experimentally in the rats.

Two physiologists at Yale University, Dr. David Lester and Dr. Leon Greenberg, proved Dr. Mardones's conclusions to be invalid. Repeating his experiments, they offered the rats a third choice—sucrose solution. The animals reduced their alcohol intake and turned to the sugar solution instead.

Genetotrophic Theory

Next to appear on the scene was the genetotrophic theory of alcoholism offered by Dr. Roger J. Williams, University of Texas biochemist. This theory, positing a nutritional deficiency resulting from an inherited (genetotrophic) metabolic defect, was little more than a restatement of Dr. Mardones's hypothesis. Dr. Williams was unable, despite several different approaches in the laboratory, to produce support for his theory. In 1959 he departed from this hypothesis and proposed instead that there is in the hypothalamus a center for the control of alcohol consumption, similar to the center for control of hunger and thirst. In certain individuals, alcohol destroys this control center, resulting in an insatiable craving for alcohol. No proof was offered.

A considerable amount of work has been conducted on this subject in the experimental laboratories of the Rutgers University Center of Alcohol Studies. In 1968 Dr. David Lester, one of the senior investigators at the center, after reviewing the work done at his laboratory and elsewhere, concluded that "the search for an inborn error of metabolism has been without profit."

Endocrine Theory

The hypothesis that alcoholism results from an endocrine disorder has been under investigation for some thirty to forty years, but there is still no evidence to support it.

In the 1950s Dr. James M. Smith, director of research on alcoholism at the New York University-Bellevue Medical Center made the startling announcement that alcoholism was caused indirectly by pituitary deficiency—that adrenal-cortex exhaustion, a secondary result of such deficiency, was in turn responsible for alcohol craving. He even proposed specific hormone treatment, stating without qualification that "it is the only treatment which offers the alcoholic prompt, specific therapy for the various phases of acute as well as chronic alcoholism." He also asserted that these deficiencies are genetic and more dominant in some ethnic groups than in others.

Dr. Smith's work and that of his followers have been criticized because of inadequate evidence, lack of controls, highly speculative conjecture concerning glandular malfunction, reasoning from conditions found in alcoholism to assumptions of glandular disorder in the prealcoholic state, and the inability to explain the absence of other signs of glandular deficiency in the presumably afflicted alcoholics.

Dr. Jellinek, who himself preferred a physical explanation of alcoholism, could not find any support for the endocrine theory: "A pre-existing, genetically determined endocrine pattern in alcoholism has not been established, nor has an initial craving for alcohol been shown by proponents of the endocrine etiological theories of alcoholism" (*Disease Concept of Alcoholism,* 1960).

Work has continued even into the 1970s in search of an endocrine cause of alcoholism. Rallying anew to this belief, Professor William Madsen, anthropologist at the University of California, summarized numerous recent experiments on this subject in *The American Alcoholic,* but was compelled to conclude that "the locus that is responsible for triggering this complex set of physiological abnormalities has not been located."

The Brain Damage Theory

It has been proposed that alcoholism may not be inborn, but rather the result of organic destruction caused by continuous contact with alcohol. A number of investigators were able to detect evidence of atrophy in the cerebral ventricles of alcoholics and guessed that this might have something to do with the increased tolerance to alcohol. This line of investigation has been fruitless.

The Metabolism Theory

There has been considerable speculation that the rate of alcohol metabolism is different in alcoholics and nonalcoholics and that such differences might somehow lead to an explanation of the alcoholic's susceptibility. This hypothesis, too, has been refuted by research. There is no significant difference between the rate of metabolism in alcoholics and nonalcoholics when they are tested after a prolonged abstinence. Prolonged alcohol intake does speed up alcohol metabolism, in nonalcoholics as well as alcoholics, but the rates return to normal in both groups when intake is reduced.

The Allergy Theory

More a popular concept than a scientific concept, the allergy theory of alcoholism holds that certain people have a peculiar body chemistry which responds to intake of small quantities of alcohol with loss of control. The only support offered by those who proposed this explanation is that in some superficial respects the physiological changes in intoxication resemble those in hay fever—since one is an allergy, then the other may well be, too. This theory has been criticized as being supported only by analogy, metaphor, and connotation. It posits a cellular basis for the craving for and habituation to alcohol, but none has been found. Furthermore, in characteristic allergy, exposure to small amounts of the toxic substance causes extreme reaction and additional quantities may cause death. With alcohol, on the other hand, ingestion of small amounts creates the desire to consume even larger amounts, producing disturbance in body functioning only when the amount consumed is so great as to interfere with fundamental biological processes.

7

Alcohol Addiction

The term *addiction* has been used in two distinct ways in regard to alcohol. In one meaning, it exclusively connotes an overpowering desire, or craving, for alcohol and the need to obtain it by any means—this and nothing more. There is no implication as to the nature of the addiction—whether it is psychological or physiological. *Alcohol addict* has been used this way to distinguish between those who can drink excessively for years without losing control of their drinking and those who have lost control.

The other meaning includes the conditions of overpowering craving and uncontrolled drinking but goes beyond, adding that alcohol addiction is an addiction in the "true pharmacological sense," that is, in the same sense as heroin, morphine, and cocaine. The implication is that when a person becomes addicted to alcohol the craving arises not only from the psyche but also from the soma, the body tissues themselves. "Something has happened to the cell metabolism," so that now alcohol is essential to the cell's vital functions. When the cells are deprived of this essential chemical, the body goes into the convulsion of withdrawal.

THE CONCEPT OF
PHYSICAL ADDICTION

The concept of alcoholism as a physical addiction in the "true pharmacological sense" was introduced by Dr. Jellinek in 1960 in his *Disease Concept of Alcoholism:* "The gamma and delta species of alcoholism show the same addictive processes, namely acquired tissue tolerance, subsequent increase in the amount required, and adaptation of cell metabolism to alcohol, evidence of which is seen in the withdrawal symptoms, which in their turn lead to the manifestation of craving, that is, physical dependence. . . . The withdrawal symptoms indicate a true physical demand for alcohol. . . . In this acute condition, it seems justified to speak of an irresistible demand or craving for alcohol."

The concept was a welcome one. It made alcoholism more understandable. Soon it gained widespread credibility and in many quarters attained the status of dogma. Yet pharmacologists themselves offer no support for the hypothesis of an alteration in cell metabolism as a result of which the tissues themselves crave the drug. On the contrary, the World Health Organization Expert Committee on Drug Dependence maintains that drug addiction is primarily psychological.

The presence of tolerance and physical dependence (withdrawal symptoms) is cited by many as evidence that alcoholism is a drug addiction "in the true pharmacological sense." Dr. Jack Mendelson, an American authority on alcoholism, states in *The Biochemical Mechanisms of Alcohol Addiction* that "alcoholism has only recently been shown to be a form of addiction defined in terms of the traditional pharmacological criteria of tolerance and dependence." Yet, the pharmacologists responsible for the position of the World Health Organization on drug dependence believe that tolerance and physical dependence are entirely incidental to and not at all necessary to the primary addictive process. Either or both may be absent in addiction. Either or both may be present without addiction.

The withdrawal syndrome is explained tentatively as a rebound reaction of the central nervous system on its release from the depressive influence of the drug. The biochemical mechanism underlying tolerance is not yet understood.

THE CONCEPT OF PSYCHIC DEPENDENCE

It is ironic that at the very same time when leaders in alcohol studies were seeking to formulate a physical theory of alcohol addiction based on the pharmacological model, leading pharmacologists were themselves turning away from the physical view and proclaiming a psychological explanation of drug addiction.

In 1964, the WHO Expert Committee on Drug Dependence proposed that the terms *addiction* and *habituation* be abandoned and that the term *drug-dependence* be substituted for both of them. Subsequently, alcohol was no longer considered separately but was considered as a dependence-producing drug, a classification which also included morphine, cocaine, and the amphetamines.

In 1965 a WHO panel on pharmacology produced "Drug Dependence: Its Significance and Characteristics," an article which appeared as a Bulletin of the World Health Organization. It included these very significant statements:

• "Individuals may become dependent upon a wide variety of chemical substances that produce central nervous system effects ranging from stimulation to depression. All of these drugs have one effect in common: they are capable of creating, in certain individuals, a particular state of mind that is termed '*psychic* dependence' [emphasis added]. In this situation there is a feeling of satisfaction and a psychic drive that requires periodic or continuous administration of the drug to produce pleasure or avoid discomfort. Indeed, this mental state is the most powerful of all the factors involved in chronic intoxication with psychotropic drugs, and with certain types of drugs it may be the only factor involved, even in the case of the most intense craving and perpetuation of compulsive abuse."

• "Some drugs also induce physical dependence which is an

adaptive state that manifests itself by intense physical disturbances when administration of the drug is suspended. . . . These disturbances, i.e., the withdrawal or abstinence syndromes, are made up of specific arrays of symptoms and signs of a psychic and physical nature that are characteristic for each drug type. Physical dependence is a powerful factor in reinforcing the influence of psychic dependence upon continuing drug use or relapse to drug use after attempted withdrawal."

• "To reiterate, *psychic dependence can and does develop, especially with stimulant-type drugs without any evidence of physical dependence* [emphasis added] and therefore without any abstinence syndrome developing after drug withdrawal. Physical dependence, too, can be induced without notable psychic dependence; indeed, physical dependence is an inevitable result of the pharmacological action of some drugs with sufficient amount and time of administration. . . ."

• "Many of the drugs that induce dependence, especially those that create physical dependence, also induce tolerance, which is an adaptive state characterized by diminished response to the same quantity of drug, or by the fact that a larger dose is required to produce the same degree of pharmacodynamic effect. *Both drug dependence and drug abuse may occur without the development of demonstrable tolerance* [emphasis added]."

Dr. Maurice H. Seevers, one of the panel of pharmacology experts that drew up the WHO statement of 1965, summarized the findings in the *Journal of the American Medical Association*: "In summary, all drug dependence has as a basis psychological conditioning to the psychopharmacological effects of chemical substances. The initiating predominant parameter which applies to all drugs, stimulants and depressants alike, is primary psychological dependence resulting from the positive reinforcement of reward. For those depressants which are capable of creating physical dependence, another parameter, secondary psychological dependence is initiated and maintained as negative and aversive reinforcement from actual or contemplated drug withdrawal."

The conditioned-reflex theory explains the development of alcohol addiction or alcohol dependence as arising from a basic pattern:

Anxiety and dejection → drinking → relief and pleasure.

This pattern is practiced over and over again and becomes established as a learned response. The drinker has other choices for the relief of anxiety, but such relief would be in the future and hence not as attractive as the immediate relief obtained from drinking. The immediate reward (relief and pleasure) reinforces drinking as a conditioned response, which progressively preempts the field of response choices, narrowing it down to just this one. Once established, the drinking response is triggered by the slightest twinge of anxiety, depression, or frustration.

The withdrawal symptoms, while physical in nature, are experienced as discomfort, pain, and terror. Having gone through them once, or having observed them in others, the drinker seeks to avoid them by continuation of drinking. This reinforces the primary conditioned reflex and intensifies the compulsive need for alcohol.

Conditioning theory also explains why the alcoholic continues to drink even though his drinking produces punishment and pain. A learned response established through reward can be extinguished if it eventually brings on punishment. Thus a child learns to reach for the cookie jar because the act ends in reward (the pleasure of eating the cookie). When his mother wants to stop the practice, she tells him "no" and emphasizes it with a slap on the hand. The pain of the mother's disapproval as well as the pain of the slap extinguish the learned response—he stops reaching for the cookie jar. But if instead of meting out immediate punishment the mother waits and scolds the child a half-hour later, or threatens not to buy him a toy for Christmas, the act will not be extinguished as easily.

In the case of the alcoholic, the punishment (the consequences of drinking) comes into play only after the drinking has stopped and therefore has little effect on the drinking response; it is too remote.

ALCOHOL AS A COPING
MECHANISM

Another explanation of the entrenchment of drinking as a fixed pattern of behavior is the psychodynamic concept of coping.

The ego is the central integrating force in the psyche. One of its major tasks is to keep in check immature, impulsive, unethical, and immoral urges and behavior. Another is to motivate the individual and enable him to do the things necessary to meet life's requirements, that is, to cope.

A person whose ego is functioning at a high level is said to have good coping capabilities or skills. The essential alcoholic has a minimum of ego-coping skills and quickly turns to alcohol for comfort, relief from frustration and failure, and escape from a reality he cannot handle. The reactive alcoholic has a good repertoire of ego-coping skills but becomes vulnerable to the use of alcohol when prolonged stress and difficulty wear down his emotional strength and control.

The essential alcoholic is likely to take to drink the first time he has to go out and support himself, or "make it" with a girl, or set up an independent existence away from his family. Since he does not have the ego-competence to persevere and endure the frustrations of disappointment and failure, or even delayed success, he quickly turns to alcohol, which becomes his escape, his self-assurance, and his self-justification.

The reactive alcoholic has managed well, but reaches a point where his ego-competence is threatened or overwhelmed, as in a crisis in marriage, breakup of a family, loss of a job and inability to find work, or inability to live up to the expectations of his mate or family. The sense of loss, hopelessness, entrapment and failure propel him toward the escape route of drinking. Once this pattern is initiated and the result found gratifying, alcohol becomes the preferred and exclusive way to deal with the problem. Eventually, the realistic measures he has used to solve his problems fall by the wayside and drinking replaces the ego as the integrating force in his life. The psyche is now maintaining itself by means of an artificial technique. The realistic regime has been exchanged for a drug regime of illusion and unreality, destroying the natural ego organization.

This would explain the insidious progression of alcoholism without having to resort to the elaborate and unsubstantiated hypothesis of an inborn physiological mechanism.

The first step is taken when a person begins using alcohol as a way of avoiding or sidestepping a problem. The problem remains unsolved, more problems are created, and an opportunity has been missed to develop problem-solving skills and coping behaviors that would enable the person to deal more effectively with future difficulties. The next time a problem arises, he is less prepared to meet it, because he has learned a maladaptive avoidance response rather than an adequate coping technique. He will again use avoidance and drinking because it is easier, and another problem will remain unsolved. Repeated avoidance produces new and compounded problems, which are met with avoidance and drinking once more. The more hopeless the situation becomes, the more the individual resorts to drinking until the point comes when things are in so bad a state, internally and externally, that he throws up his hands and gives himself over to drinking as his only means of survival.

8

The Influence of Heredity

Whether alcoholism is regarded as a psychological or physical disorder, the question of heredity is still pertinent. The psychological cluster of traits which are said to predispose an individual to the need for alcohol could be genetically determined in whole or in part, as are some traits of temperament and some psychiatric illnesses. Should a genetic factor be found to be operating in the manifestation of these traits, it could be said that the psychological susceptibility to alcohol, or alcohol vulnerability, is inherited.

If alcoholism is proved to be the result of a physiological or organic defect related to a genetic factor, it could be said that the physical predisposition to alcohol is inherited.

There are several methods for investigating whether a trait is inherited or acquired: family studies, twin studies, adoption studies, and genetic marker studies.

FAMILY STUDIES

When a trait is found "running in the family," it is reasonable to assume that the gene for this particular trait was introduced into the family several generations back and then distributed throughout the family tree by grandchildren and great-grandchildren of the introducer. This is true with such traits as blue eyes, snub nose, short or tall stature. It would also be true for such physical disorders as colorblindness, sickle cell anemia, hemophilia, and familial polyposis (a precancerous condition of the bowels). There is also evidence that there is a genetic factor operating in heart disease, diabetes, schizophrenia, breast cancer, and other types of cancer.

Without question, alcoholism, too, is a "familial disease." It definitely does "run in the family." In *Heredity and Alcohol* (1945), Dr. Jellinek summarized the results of a number of earlier studies embracing some 4,000 alcoholics. He found that 52 percent of these subjects had one or two alcoholic parents. Several other studies conducted during the past 35 years have produced additional evidence that a very high proportion of alcoholics have an alcoholic father, mother, brother, sister, or a combination of these.

These findings may certainly be regarded as evidence that something is being transmitted from parents to children which influences them to become alcoholics. But this "something" need not be genetic. It could very well be environmental. The son or daughter could be imitating a parent. The ethos of the family or culture might recommend drinking as a way of dealing with life's problems —or as a way of life. The social and economic conditions in which the family finds itself might be so difficult that alcohol is seen as the only escape route available to parents and offspring alike.

Some family studies, however, point to the existence of familial tendencies which would be difficult to attribute to environmental influences. In his study on heredity, Dr. Jellinek learned that 35 percent of the alcoholics had a tendency to deviance in common with the parents in the form of psychiatric disabilities. In 1956, the Swiss psychiatrist Dr. Manfred Bleuler, in a study of the families of a substantial number of psychiatric patients, found that the percentage of alcoholics in this group was much higher than in the population at large. He concluded, quite in agreement with Dr. Jellinek, that "the genetics of alcoholism are closely related to the genetics of abnormal personality development."

A recent review of familial tendencies in alcoholism by the American psychiatrists Dr. Donald W. Goodwin and Dr. Samuel

B. Guze supports this view. There is preponderant evidence for an excess of abnormal personality and antisocial behavior in the families of alcoholics.

TWIN STUDIES

Since identical twins share exactly the same genes (as is evidenced by their identical appearance) it is assumed that any trait, if it is hereditary, will appear in exactly the same form in both twins. If alcoholism is hereditary it would be expected to occur in both members of an identical twin pair if it occurs in either. One way to determine whether alcoholism is inherited would be to identify a substantial number of alcoholics who are also members of identical twin pairs and then to discover whether the corresponding twins are also alcoholics. A high concordance would point to the existence of a hereditary trait; no-higher-than-chance concordance would indicate the opposite.

The studies most frequently cited are those of Dr. Lennart Kaij, psychiatrist at the University of Lund, Sweden, and Dr. Juha Partanen, statistician, and his colleagues at the Finnish Foundation for Alcohol Studies, Helsinki. Dr. Kaij located 174 male twin pairs (some identical, some fraternal), in which at least one of the members had been convicted for some infraction of the law resulting from excessive drinking. There was no information available as to whether these subjects had been diagnosed as alcoholic, but the conviction was regarded as sufficient evidence. Using this criterion, Dr. Kaij found a 54-percent concordance among the identical twins compared to a 28-percent concordance among the fraternal twins. This is certainly supportive evidence for a hereditary factor in alcoholism.

Dr. Partanen studied a group of 902 male twin pairs with respect to drinking habits and consequences of drinking (such as arrests for drunkenness and for family and job difficulties). He found no difference between the identical and fraternal twins with respect to the consequences of drinking, the criterion Dr. Kaij had used. There was considerable difference, however, with respect to heavy and frequent drinking. The concordance among identical twins was high, among fraternal twins, low. The identical twins also had high concordance for total abstinence.

Both studies at least indicate that there is a genetic factor in operation predisposing some people more than others to excessive drinking. The fact that this is associated with disturbing personal and social consequences in one cultural sample and not in another may or may not be the result of different social standards for personal restraint and control in the two cultures.

ADOPTION STUDIES

Adoption studies seek out children who have been raised away from their biological parents and are therefore presumed to be free of the environmental influences of their parents' home. If in spite of this separation the adopted children manifest, in large degree, traits found in their parents, it is assumed that these traits have been transmitted genetically.

The first adoption study on alcoholism was reported in 1944 by Dr. Anna Roe, a Yale University psychologist, who studied the cases of 61 children who had been placed in foster homes before the age of 10. Twenty-five came from nonalcoholic parents. Thirty-six had at least one alcoholic parent. Of the children with an alcoholic parent or parents, not one became an alcoholic and only three used alcohol regularly, indicating no hereditary factor in alcoholism. These conclusions have been criticized on the ground that the sample was too small and that it included a large proportion of females. Since women are less likely to become alcoholics than men, this would tend to bias the findings.

More recently Dr. Marc A. Schukit and his associates at the Washington University School of Medicine, St. Louis, studied the cases of a number of individuals who had been separated from an alcoholic parent and placed with a surrogate parent. A substantial proportion of these children became alcoholics. Sixty-two percent of those who became alcoholics had come from an alcoholic biological parent, compared to only 20 percent of a group of children who did not have an alcoholic biological parent. If a child had an alcoholic biological parent, it made little difference in the outcome whether he was placed with a surrogate parent who was or was not an alcoholic—his chances of becoming an alcoholic were the same. This study suggests the persistence of a genetic factor which operates regardless of environmental circumstances.

A more exhaustive study was conducted in Denmark by a team of American and Danish scientists headed by Dr. Goodwin. From a pool of 15,000 adoptees, 55 male subjects were identified who had at least one parent who had been hospitalized for alcoholism, had been separated from their biological parents before they were six weeks old, and had never had contact with them again. The members of this group were then matched with controls who were like them in every important respect except for having an alcoholic parent. Of the group of 55 (those with an alcoholic parent) 18 percent had become alcoholics; of the controls, only 5 percent were alcoholics.

In a follow-up study, Dr. Goodwin was able to take his investigation one step further. Twenty men in the group of 55 had a brother who had remained with the parents and had been brought up by them. There were as many alcoholics among the sons who had been adopted as there were among those who had remained with the alcoholic parent. Both studies argue for a genetic factor in alcoholism.

GENETIC MARKER STUDIES

Certain human diseases are associated with others through chromosomal linkage. It is known, for example, that people with Down's syndrome (mongolism) have a high risk for leukemia, and that people with hemophilia are quite frequently colorblind. Following this lead, a number of investigators have sought to learn whether there is an association between alcoholism and such markers as colorblindness and blood types. The genetic marker (or genetic linkage) studies on alcoholism have been reviewed thoroughly by Dr. Goodwin. They are contradictory and produce little evidence of any significance relating alcoholism to any specific biological factor.

It may be said in conclusion that a genetic factor does appear to be operating in alcoholism but that it appears to be concerned with psychological factors which predispose the individual to use alcohol rather than to a biological trait of alcoholism.

9

Ethnic and Other Cultural Influences

In addition to the familial influences, genetic and environmental, which operate in producing individual vulnerability to alcohol, another set of factors comes into play: the attitudes toward drinking and the drinking practices of the culture, particularly those having to do with the use of drinking as a means of dealing with one's problems. Those factors have as yet been only superficially explored, but what is already known provides valuable insights.

DRINKING IN THE UNITED STATES

According to a recent survey, approximately two out of every three Americans over 21 drink (68 percent); about one out of three abstains (32 percent). More men drink than women (77 to 60 percent). The percentage of drinkers is highest for those in the highest socieconomic brackets (83 percent) and lowest for those in the lowest brackets (51 percent).

Among the religious denominations, Jews are at the top of the list (92 percent), followed closely by Episcopalians (91 percent). Baptists are at the bottom of the list (47 percent); in between are Catholics (83 percent), Lutherans (81 percent), Presbyterians (75 percent), and Methodists (66 percent).

Regionally, the Middle Atlantic and New England states have the highest percentages of drinkers (83 and 79 percent), the East South Central states the lowest (35 percent). Drinking is heaviest in the large cities and urban areas, lightest in the rural areas.

When *heavy* drinking is considered, rather than just drinking, the picture changes considerably. Heavy drinking was measured in this survey by an index combining quantity, frequency, and variability. A typical heavy drinker would be one who drinks every day and occasionally drinks five drinks or more at a time; or one who drinks at least weekly, taking five or more drinks on most occasions.

In the population as a whole, aged 21 and over, 12 percent are heavy drinkers. Males outnumber females four to one. There is very little difference in the rate of heavy drinking between the upper and lower socioeconomic brackets. In the upper third, the proportion of heavy drinkers is about 13 percent; in the lowest third, about 11 percent.

Among the religious denominations, Catholics have the highest percentage of heavy drinkers (19 percent), followed by Lutherans (15 percent), Episcopalians (12 percent), Presbyterians (12 percent), Methodists (10 percent), Jews (10 percent), and Baptists (7 percent).

Comparison by ethnic grouping shows that 30 percent of the black population abstains, compared with 31 percent of the white population. The heavy-drinking rate for blacks is 14 percent; for whites, 12 percent.

DRINKING PATTERNS AMONG ITALIANS

Americans of Italian extraction, it has been found, drink a great deal but not many become alcoholics. Almost invariably, population samples of alcoholics (in psychiatric hospitals, in police arrests, in social agency contacts) show disproportionally low rates for Italian-Americans.

A study by Dr. Giorgio Lolli, an American psychiatrist, has revealed that there are very few teetotalers among Italian-Americans and that, despite the stereotype, only a handful (2 to 4 percent) drink wine exclusively. The great majority drink (and abundantly) beer, whiskey, and aperitifs as well as wine. Also, contrary to stereotype, they do not drink mainly with their meals. They drink socially and "for the effect," even in the course of an ordinary day. They give strong approval to drinking, even by children (wine), and it is a common practice to initiate the children early, with tastes and sips of wine. An occasional drunkenness is accepted with tolerance, but not condoned.

Significantly, there is this progression: Italians in Italy drink wine almost exclusively, drink it with their meals, drink for "health and custom," very seldom become intoxicated. First-generation Italians in America drink a little less wine, a little more distilled spirits, and more frequently away from the table. They report a somewhat higher percentage of intoxication than do their countrymen. Second and third generations drink much less wine, much more distilled spirits, much more on social occasions, and report a much higher frequency of intoxication.

DRINKING PATTERNS AMONG JEWS

Jews, too, drink a great deal but produce not many alcoholics. The older generations confine much of their drinking (wine as well as distilled spirits) to the home, to religious rituals, and to celebrations (weddings, circumcisions, bar mitzvahs). Members of the younger generation of middle-class Jews drink like other middle-class Americans—at cocktail parties, receptions, business lunches, and other social gatherings.

Considerable attention is also given to the ritual and religious role of wine among Jews. Drinking of wine plays an integral role in the special blessings attending virtually every religious observance and holiday. Wine is drunk during the Passover seders and is generally available throughout the Passover holiday.

Excessive drinking is inversely related to the degree of adherence to Orthodox practice (strictest in ritual observance). As Orthodoxy declines, intoxication increases in both frequency and intensity, converging in extent with the norms of the larger society. The more observant Jews are characteristically sober despite the widespread and frequent use of alcoholic beverages, especially wine and spirits.

Drinking in general is neither shunned nor advocated in the Jewish culture. It is taken casually as a part of normal living. Drunkenness and excessive drinking are, however, abominated. Many Jews indicate that they have been brought up with the notion that drunkenness is a Gentile vice, sobriety a Jewish virtue. This is consistent with the Jewish abhorrence of violence and loss of emotional control, which Jews associate with the persecution to which they have been subjected over the centuries. This strongly internalized rejection of heavy drinking cannot help but exert an influence in keeping the rate of alcoholism low.

Dr. Charles R. Snyder, an American sociologist who has gone deeply into the cultural influences affecting drinking, makes this most profound observation, in an article entitled "Culture and Jewish Sobriety": "Where drinking is integrated with the process of socialization and the central social symbolism and rites of the group, norms of sobriety can be sustained and pathologies are rare."

DRINKING PATTERNS
AMONG THE CHINESE

Dr. Snyder's observation on drinking patterns among Jews in America appears to apply to the Chinese as well. In a study of drinking among the Chinese-Americans in New York City, Dr. Milton Barnett, Cornell University anthropologist, found that drinking of wine and distilled spirits was widespread but that there was not much intoxication and very little alcoholism. Whatever alcoholism there was appeared to be concentrated among a few old men who lived and drank in isolation.

Wine and spirits are drunk within the family and in ceremonies related to birth, birthdays, weddings, and rites for the dead; also in national and religious celebrations and at social and festive gatherings. Within the home and at social gatherings, drinking represents an important social function, almost a ritual.

Little boys are introduced early to drinking, casually, but not with encouragement. This appears to foster a permissiveness, together with the development of a set of attitudes which sanction drinking socially but disapprove of intoxication.

Intoxication is deplored, and the transgressor is ridiculed. The loss of face acts as a potent deterrent toward repeated episodes. Women drink only after marriage and are excluded from the drinking ritual in the home. Drunkenness in a woman is treated much more severely than drunkenness in men. When intoxication does occur, it is generally quiet and soporific, rarely explosive and violent. The only expression of aggression is loquaciousness and expansive behavior, almost never overt hostility.

DRINKING PATTERNS AMONG THE IRISH

By comparison with the Italians, Jews, and Chinese in America, the Irish stand out as an ethnic group in which there is a great deal of drinking, frequent drunkenness, and a high rate of alcoholism. In almost every table showing rates of drinking problems and of alcoholism, the Irish in America are at or very near the top.

Heavy drinking and drinking as a way to deal with one's problems have their origin in the folk customs of the Irish in Ireland, dating back at least to the 18th century and possibly further. The Irish have had a long and picturesque history with alcohol, a history in which alcohol has penetrated deeply into nearly every aspect of social life. In *Attitudes Toward Drinking in the Irish Culture,* Dr. Robert Bales, an American sociologist, delves into the literature pertaining to Irish drinking customs in the 19th century and produces some telling comments: "After the baptism, a Christening party is in order . . . and whiskey is liberally provided. The family's status is at stake in this matter and niggardliness in amount and quality of whiskey is avoided. . . . Among the Irish Catholics, drink is the symptom for hospitality. It stands alone and is not associated with food. . . . The middle-aged farmer or laborer in Ireland will start for fair or market at 4 or 5 a.m. and when his business is done, at noon, will go straight to a public house and stay drinking . . . until 8 or 9 in the evening, when he leaves for home hopelessly drunk, not having taken a morsel of food all day. . . . From infancy, the Irish child of the 19th century saw a great deal of drinking by both males and females, older and younger, and early began to participate himself. . . . An emotional difficulty of young men is believed best treated by advising them to 'drink it off.' Drowning one's sorrow becomes the accepted means of relief. . . . Drinking in clubs, hotels and saloons affords the chief social life of the men and the chief means of getting them out of homes dominated by their women. . . . The habit of 'treating' is a social law in Catholic Ireland, enforced with the vigor of a Coercion Act. If a man happens to be in a public house alone, and if any of his acquaintances come in, no matter how many, it is his duty to 'stand' the drinks. . . . Then if there are half a dozen men in the company, each insists on 'standing' drinks all around. . . . It is a deadly insult to refuse a drink."

The Irish who emigrated to this country during the last hundred years carried many of these customs with them, and wherever they remain a cohesive cultural group, retaining their identification with the old country and its folkways, the practical and symbolic importance of drinking persists.

Dr. Bales notes that among the Irish, in contrast with the Jews, there is no ritual drinking. A good deal of the drinking in which the individual participates almost from the beginning to the end of his life cycle is convivial as well as utilitarian. Drinking is used as a medicine for physical ills of all sorts. It is employed to assuage hunger, pacify guilt, get warm, relieve sexual and aggressive tension, dispel fatigue, and promote sleep. It serves to relieve emotional burdens ranging from minor disappointments to deep grief. All these uses, says Dr. Bales, are built into the fabric of Irish culture and through that channel into the fabric of Irish feeling, thinking and behavior.

In their study on Boston area boys who had become alcoholics, the McCords noted that the predictive factor of dependency conflict was found to exist in a high degree among the youth of Irish extraction.

The influence of dependency conflict, the use of drinking as a way of asserting masculinity, the prevalance of drinking as a social custom, and the preferred use of drinking as a way of dealing with one's problems may all be presumed to contribute to the high rate of alcoholism among the Irish in America.

DRINKING PATTERNS AMONG AMERICAN INDIANS

Among the many myths concerning ethnic drinking practices, the one that has persisted most stubbornly, even among the subjects themselves, is the firewater myth. According to this belief, the American Indian is constitutionally prone to an inordinate craving for alcohol and to go wildly out of control when he is drinking.

To learn whether or not this notion has validity, Dr. Joy Leland, research anthropologist at the University of Nevada, reviewed the extensive literature on the subject, anecdotal as well as scientific, and concluded that the firewater myth is indeed a myth. With some variations, the American Indian responds to alcohol very much like other Americans. Where the tribal customs stress constraint and control, reaction to alcohol tends to be subdued. Where they do not, it tends to be unrestrained. As with drinkers of other ethnic groups, the extent of the reaction is related to the amount consumed, the setting in which the drinking is done, the force of social restraints, and other cultural factors. The American Indian does not have an inordinate craving for alcohol, nor does he respond explosively after the consumption of just a small quantity of alcohol, or more so than others after consumption of large quantities.

Dr. Leland also inquired into the validity of a reverse firewater myth which has taken hold among social scientists, the belief that there is an extraordinarily low rate of alcoholism among American Indians. The data were conflicting and inconclusive.

Much has been made of the fact that American Indians and racial groups with whom they are presumed to have some evolutionary relationship respond differently to alcohol from whites. Some studies have shown that Eskimos and American Indians have lower rates of alcohol metabolism than whites, a difference that could not be accounted for by diet or other experience, and that Mongolians respond with flushing and mild intoxication to doses of alcohol that do not affect whites. Even if these differences are truly genetic, they indicate nothing about higher or lower susceptibility to alcoholism.

There is, however, a high degree of problem drinking among many American Indian tribes. Drinking-related crimes are many times higher among Indians than among the population as a whole. Characteristically, it is reported, a number of young males get together in a group or gang, drink heavily, and then engage in disorderly as well as criminal behavior.

In *Problem Drinking Among American Indians,* anthropologist Edward P. Dozier noted that by virtue of considerable intermarriage with non-Indian stock, the American Indian can no longer be regarded as a pure biological group and that the roots of problem drinking must be sought in historical, social, and cultural circumstances. These he identifies as economic and social deprivation, rejection by white society as inferiors, deterioration of traditional customs and institutions, and a high level of anxiety.

Comparison is made between the Klamath Indians of Oregon, who have a high rate of drinking-related crimes, and the Pueblo Indians of New Mexico and Arizona, who have a low rate. Among the former, Dr. Dozier points out, economic suffering is widespread and traditional social and religious practices are all but extinct. Among the latter, religious and social customs are well preserved and the basic means of subsistence, farming, is well maintained.

DRINKING PATTERNS AMONG BLACKS IN AMERICA

In whatever settings they have been studied—the general hospital, the psychiatric clinic, the state mental hospital, the community at large—blacks in the United States have shown rates of alcoholism two to five times as high as those for whites. Problem drinking—drinking associated with disorder, violence, automobile accidents, and crime—has also been consistently higher for blacks than for whites.

Alcoholism has its onset much earlier among blacks than among whites, and the ratio of female alcoholics to male alcoholics is higher.

Heavy drinking and intoxication are pervasive in urban black populations. In a study on safety in the Midwest, thousands of drivers were stopped at random and breath-tested for blood alcohol levels. Blood level rates indicating intoxication were five times as great among blacks as among whites.

Heavy drinking starts much earlier among black youth than among white. Even in the relatively "safe" setting of the free all-black college, heavy drinking and intoxication is very much higher, starting in the freshman classes, than it is in all-white colleges, and the character of the drinking is different. Black youths drink more to modify reality than to socialize, and intoxication and drinking to unconsciousness are present in excess.

There is considerable difference in the patterns of drinking and drinking-related problems between upper- and lower-class blacks. Middle-class blacks drink mostly in their homes and in cocktail lounges, and both men and women drink considerably less than their lower-class counterparts. The poor drink in friendship groups at home, in the tavern, or on the streets. Sociability and companionship are a very important factor in their drinking; however, they also have a high record of arrests for intoxication and disorderly conduct associated with drinking.

Considering the social and economic conditions in which blacks in America live today, it is almost redundant to look for the causes of excessive drinking and alcoholism. From childhood on they are exposed to the deprivations and frustrations imposed by the larger society and to the attendant sense of inadequacy, futility, and insecurity; they also endure to a much greater degree than whites the traumatic experiences which have been found to be antecedents to escape drinking and alcoholism—deviant parental models, disrupted families, school dropouts, and delinquency.

There is no evidence that drinking is especially recommended among blacks as a means of dealing with problems, but it hardly needs a recommendation as so few other ways are available. Since response choices are so few, it is understandable that the drinking response quickly preempts the field and that the rewards of relief and escape provided by alcohol produce alcoholism.

DRINKING PATTERNS
IN FRANCE

While Americans of French descent do not present a distinct drinking pattern, the drinking patterns in France itself are of interest because of its fame as a wine-producing country. An in-depth study conducted by Dr. Roland Sadoun and his associates has disclosed that about 90 percent of the adult population of France drinks. Beer, distilled spirits, and aperitifs account for only a small part of the drinking: wine represents at least 90 percent of the total. The average daily intake of wine is about three-fifths of a quart for men and about one-fifth of a quart for women. The range for drinkers is from one glass to two quarts or more a day. Thirty-six percent of the population drink a quart or more. Farm workers drink considerably more than white-collar workers and executives. The poor consume much larger quantities of wine than the well-to-do.

About 85 percent of the wine-drinking takes place with meals.

Between-meal drinking is more common among the working people than among executives and professionals. Most of the wine-drinking is done at home. Manual workers, farm workers, and domestic workers account for much of the drinking that goes on at places of work or in cafes.

Alcoholism in France appears to be high, by comparison with most Western countries, but the prevailing attitude among the French is that wine is nourishing and strengthening and that the working man needs it to enable him to perform his arduous duties. The attitude toward distilled spirits is much less tolerant: the majority consider whiskey to be harmful.

10

The Marriage Partner
of the Alcoholic

Current psychological theory, evolving from family therapy, sees the family not only as the victim of the alcoholic but also as the breeding ground in which alcoholism sprouts and thrives. A husband or wife does not create alcoholism in a spouse. The prospective alcoholic comes into the situation already predisposed to the use of alcohol for relief and escape. The spouse does nothing more than provide half the ingredients for a two-way struggle which exacerbates the susceptible individual's anxiety and low self-esteem, entangles the partner in a situation from which he or she does not have the strength to escape, and drives him or her to the only possible outlet—alcohol.

The family conflict formula that spawns alcoholism in one family is the same as the one that produces depression, anxiety neurosis, obsessive-compulsive neurosis, paranoia, sexual acting-out, and other aberrations in other families. The only difference is in the choice of symptoms: it is the conflict and entrapment that cause the breakdown; the form of breakdown is determined by the particular nature of the person's pre-existing vulnerabilities.

Neurotic people come into a marriage with neurotic needs, to dominate or be dominated, to punish or be punished, to mother or be mothered, to control or be controlled, to humiliate or be humiliated. So long as these needs are mutually fulfilled, there is pleasure, contentment, and peace. It is on this basis that many "good" marriages are made.

However, each neurotic individual has many different kinds of needs. Some may complement the partner's, others may create conflict. Attraction and liking may occur because one set of needs is complementary; antagonism and dislike may develop because of the conflict of another set.

For example, a man and a woman may attract each other because they are both physically appealing and because both have an excessive need to be admired. The conquest of one attractive person by another proves to both of them how attractive they are, thus boosting their self-esteem and satisfying their narcissism. However, one may be a clinging person in need of constant mothering and attention and the other may find intimate relationships frightening and intolerable. The more the first fights for closeness the more the other struggles against it. Or it may be that both have an extraordinary need to be mothered and neither has much capacity for mothering. Consequently, each will be demanding from the other something neither is able to give.

In any such situation resentment, hurt, rejection, anger, retaliation, and revenge are inevitable. The chances that the relationship will work out depend on the balance of forces. If there is considerable satisfaction from mutual admiration, sex, children, social activities, and entertainment, the conflict might be pushed into the background and the relationship prove satisfactory. This is in fact what happens in many marriages until something comes along to alter the balance, such as the growing up of the children, a financial reverse, a serious illness, or a death in the family.

When the equilibrium is upset and no other is established, strife and struggle persist. The woman undercuts the man in his role of husband, father, sex partner, competent male; the man undercuts the woman in her role of mother, wife, sex partner, homemaker; they both undercut each other's self-esteem. Ultimately one of the partners begins to break down, to sink into repressed rage, apathy, helplessness, and depression. If that partner happens to have the traits that predispose a person to alcoholism, that is the form the breakdown will take.

A legend has developed that the wife of the alcoholic is a certain type of person who marries an alcoholic to satisfy her own needs, works consciously or unconsciously against his recovery so as to keep him as he is, and "decompensates," that is, develops clinical symptoms of neurosis, psychosomatic illness, and even psychosis should he get better.

This legend grew out of the untested observations of a few professionals working with a limited number of cases. Detecting certain personality traits in the wives of some of their alcoholic clients or patients, they attributed these traits to wives of alcoholics as a whole.

One writer confidently identified four distinct types: Suffering Susan, Controlling Catherine, Wavering Winifred, and Punitive Polly. Because of their novelty and imaginativeness, these generalizations caught the fancy of other professionals, came into use in professional circles, and found their way into folklore by way of the mass media.

It is only recently that these reports, based on observation, were challenged by controlled scientific studies. The results of these studies, numbering in the dozens and spanning some 15 years, have been summarized by Patricia Edwards, of the Alberta Alcoholism and Drug Abuse Commission, and her colleagues:

"The classic clinical description propounded between 1937 and 1959 of the wives of alcoholics as aggressive domineering women who married to mother or control a man has been demonstrated to be inaccurate. Further, none of these researchers were able to establish the existence of a personality type unique to or characteristic of alcoholics' wives.

"An assumption derived from the classic view of the wives of alcoholics was that because such wives had such a great investment in their husband's alcoholism, they would 'decompensate,' that is, their personalities would deteriorate if their husbands became abstinent. Later studies found that wives tend to improve rather than deteriorate when their husbands become abstinent.

"*In all of this, these women seem much like other women ex-*

periencing marital problems [emphasis added]."

It is not only in marriages involving an alcoholic (male or female) that a person picks a mate who will fulfill his or her neurotic needs; it is true in all marriages in which one or both partners have such needs to fulfill.

Alcoholism is only incidental in this matchmaking process: the important ingredients are the personality characteristics and neurotic needs of each partner and the extent to which the personality traits of each satisfy the neurotic requirements of the other. Since in most cases the alcoholism does not show up until months or years after the marriage, it cannot have been a factor.

The choice of spouse to fill a particular requirement is by no means conscious. Each senses in the other the susceptible or desired qualities, and attraction ensues. This sensing takes place on an unconscious level and is based on long years of practice, starting in childhood, in selecting personal affiliations and social situations congenial to the individual's personality requirements.

11

Basic Dogmas Are
Challenged

There has been evident in recent years a growing challenge to the solidly entrenched dogmas: that alcoholism is inevitably progressive to the point of deterioration; that there can be no remission or abatement; that an alcoholic can never return to moderate drinking; that the alcoholic is without power to decide whether or not to drink at all; and that he is unable to limit the amount he drinks once he starts drinking.

The first challenge was posed in 1962 in the form of a report that a number of treated alcoholics had returned to moderate drinking. Dr. D. L. Davies, chief of psychiatry at the Maudsley Hospital in London, reported that of 93 alcoholics who had been treated there for alcoholism, seven were found on follow-up to have been drinking socially for continuous periods from 7 to 11 years after discharge. None of these seven had been drunk in the follow-up period and all were better adjusted socially than prior to admission.

Dr. Davies's report was subjected to critical analysis by several experts and they were skeptical, since in their own experience with thousands of alcoholics none could recall a single case of resumption of normal drinking after recovery.

In 1966 Dr. R. E. Kendell, also of Maudsley Hospital, reported that of 62 patients who had been referred to the hospital and had been left to their own resources after refusing treatment there, five had returned to normal drinking on six-to-seven-year follow-up.

Shortly thereafter, Dr. Margaret E. Bailey of Columbia University cited her own experience in this area, reporting that six alcoholics whom she had interviewed repeatedly over a five-year period had been able to free themselves of alcoholism and return to moderate drinking.

In 1969 Dr. Davies and his associates produced four more such cases. Anticipating the criticism that since their patients had been able to return to normal drinking they could not really have been "true alcoholics," these investigators were careful to point out that their patients had met the strictest definitions of alcoholism by any standards.

At the Rutgers Center of Alcohol Studies, sociologist Merton Hyman made a study of 25 alcoholics 15 years after their cases had been closed in an alcoholism clinic in New Jersey. Five had reverted to steady but not excessive daily drinking, two to light occasional drinking, and one to weekend drinking. Six were totally abstinent and two were abstinent except for occasional, severe relapses. The remaining nine had continued to drink in an uncontrolled, alcoholic pattern, but there was little evidence of the "inevitable progression to total deterioration." It was remarkable, said the investigator, that several of the nine were still functioning at a somewhat effective level, with the acceptance and support of their families.

Simultaneously, accounts began to emerge of what appeared to be spontaneous remission from alcoholism by alcoholics who had had no contact at all with treatment. The best documentation came from Washington University in St. Louis. In 1959 a group of psychiatrists there interviewed some 223 soon-to-be-released felons, 93 of whom gave unequivocal histories of alcoholism. When all 93 were interviewed again ten years later, 38 were either in total remission or had had no serious drinking problem within the two-year period prior to the interview.

Attention has also been drawn to a related phenomenon, the sharp drop in the number of people treated for alcoholism after the age of 50. An Australian psychiatrist, Dr. Leslie R. H. Drew, noted that this occurred not only in his own country but throughout the world. He also observed that prognosis in the treatment of alcoholism improves after the age of 40. From this evidence he came to the tentative conclusion that many alcoholics recover spontaneously with age and that this recovery is attributable to maturity, social withdrawal, decreasing drive, and reduced social pressures.

A similar evaluation was made by Dr. E. Mansell Pattison, psychiatrist at the University of California. In an exhaustive evaluation of the treatment and rehabilitation of the alcoholic, Dr. Pattison observed that "the widespread notion of a progression is not supported by clinical and experimental data." Surveys of nontreated alcoholics in the community, he said, indicate that the progression is by no means uniform or inexorable. "In fact alcoholics may vary in time in the degree of alcoholism and move in and out of alcoholism."

Intrigued by the evidence from epidemiological studies, groups of research workers in different parts of the country conducted experiments in controlled situations to answer the question, If alcoholics are given as much alcohol as they want will they consume it all and drink themselves into oblivion?

Psychiatrist Edward Gottheil and his associates ran a series of experiments in the alcoholism treatment unit of a Veterans Administration hospital in Coatesville, Pennsylvania. While the experiments varied in some detail they followed the same basic formula: The alcoholics were allowed to drink two ounces of 86-proof alcohol every hour during the day, every day except weekends. The experiments ran from four to six weeks. In four different experiments, the results were almost identical, and striking. At least a third of the alcoholics drank nothing at all. Another third, approximately, started drinking but then gave it up before the four- or six-week period was over. Of the remaining third, a substantial proportion drank sporadically—not consistently—during the four-to-six-week period.

To account for this totally unexpected behavior of the alcoholic —the indifference to liquor when it is made available, without charge, in the hospital setting—Dr. Gottheil observed that patients in the hospital milieu reported feeling relaxed and completely free of the recurrent thoughts of drinking they experienced at home. Following discharge, however, "previously established cues became operative and the patients resumed drinking."

Psychiatrist Alfonso Paredes and his colleagues conducted an experiment designed to answer a related question: Can alcoholics control their intake of alcohol, starting and stopping when they want, or is the hold of the addiction or compulsion so great that it renders the alcoholic totally helpless to make his own decision? The research workers recruited thirty alcoholics in the alcoholism treatment unit of an Oklahoma state mental hospital and told them they would be given alcohol as part of a treatment program. Those chosen were then transferred to a separate unit in an open ward of the hospital. They had complete freedom to move about the grounds, leave the grounds, and visit neighboring bars if they chose to. Authorized drinking was done on two successive days, preceded and followed by two weeks of total abstinence. On the two test days, the subjects were offered a drink an hour from 1:30 p.m. to 10:00 p.m.

A few dropped out of the experiment. All who remained stayed sober the first two weeks and the last two weeks, even though they had the opportunity to leave and drink at the local bars. All drank when they were told they could and stopped when they were told to stop at the end of the two-day test period. None manifested, while drinking, any of the unruly, provocative, or obstinate behavior characteristic of intoxicated alcoholics in a community setting.

Dr. Paredes observed that drinking does not set off a chain reaction of drinking to oblivion, that the alcoholic can control his intake, when asked to, and that when social pressures and expectations of the outside world are absent the alcoholic does not find it necessary to drink.

He noted also that the social milieu inside the hospital was friendly and supportive compared to what the alcoholic would find on the outside. It included group classrooms and group solidarity. The consequences of drinking—sickness, punishment and ostracism—were absent. There was no criticism or nagging about drinking; it was accepted. The bar and neighborhood drinking buddies were not there. The patient was encouraged to improve his self-image by taking responsibility for his behavior. He was trusted, accepted, welcomed, and treated like an adult.

Even in a Skid Row setting, Dr. Paredes pointed out, the drinking of the alcoholic is not absolute. He will drink in some settings and not in others. His drinking pattern changes from setting to setting. The closer he comes to being exposed to conventional social demands, the more likely he is to drink. When life is suddenly structured for him, as in the hospital, mission, or recovery house, the need for alcohol is not so compelling and he is less likely to drink.

The experiments performed by Dr. Gottheil and Dr. Paredes were of the fixed-interval variety; that is, the alcoholics were offered a limited amount of alcohol on an hourly basis. This was done to conform to a technical experimental requirement. The results are no different, however, when the alcoholic has so much alcohol available that he can, if he wishes, drink himself into a stupor.

Dr. Nancy Mello, of the National Center for the Prevention and Control of Alcoholism, conducted an experiment in which alcoholics could earn tokens by performing some problem-solving tasks and then with these tokens buy as much liquor as they wished. Together, the subjects could accumulate a large supply from which each could draw freely.

Dr. Mello found that, although there was nothing to stop any of the subjects from drinking himself into insensibility, none of them attempted to do so. They were satisfied to drink just enough to achieve mild intoxication. Only small quantities—one or two ounces—were consumed at a time. Many of the subjects were able, at will, to initiate and maintain periods of total abstinence over a thirty-day period.

Controlled experiments have also demonstrated that alcoholics can learn, under laboratory conditions, to give up compulsive drinking and adopt moderate drinking habits.

Dr. Kenneth C. Mills, a psychologist, re-created in the alcoholism treatment unit of a state mental hospital in California an exact replica of a cocktail lounge, with polished bar, mirror, bottle display, music, bartender. The subjects in the experiment, all alcoholics, were told they were going to be trained to develop appropriate drinking behavior; to drink mixed rather than straight drinks, to sip rather than gulp, and to have a maximum of three drinks, each with an ounce of 86-proof alcohol in it. Drinking was thus put in a socially acceptable setting and the alcoholic encouraged to drink in a socially acceptable way.

Each subject had an electrode attached to a finger. If he took a straight drink or gulped his drink, he received a small shock. If he both drank it straight and gulped it, he received a large shock. If he asked for a fourth drink, he received a very large shock. He could avoid all shocks by drinking mixed drinks in a leisurely fashion and stopping at three.

Four of the subjects learned the moderate response the first day and sustained it for the rest of the experiment. The other nine learned it in a period of 9 to 14 days and sustained it. The researcher concluded that, in a hospital setting at least, a confirmed alcoholic can be taught to drink in the same manner as social drinkers.

A similar experiment was conducted by an Australian psychologist, Dr. S. H. Lovibond. The subjects were first taught to judge the alcohol level in their blood by a rather simple process taking a short time to learn. After they had mastered this technique they were told they could drink as much as they wanted but could not exceed a blood alcohol level of 0.065, an amount that would not produce intoxication. They were being taught, in effect, to stop when they had "had enough." If they exceeded the prescribed blood level, they received a shock on the face and neck. Of 31 patients, 21 were completely successful in developing this moderate-drinking pattern for from 16 to 60 weeks. The subjects experienced a loss of the desire to drink after having had the first two or three drinks. This experiment produced convincing refutation of the theories of loss of control, inexorable compulsion, and inevitable progression.

The training methods used by Dr. Mills and Dr. Lovibond come under the heading of aversive conditioning. Another training method developed in behavior therapy is known as operant conditioning. Like aversive conditioning, it works to eliminate an undesirable behavior by means of a relearning process. In aversive conditioning, the behavior is extinguished by transferring to it the aversion originally produced by electric shock or drugs; operant conditioning focuses on the consequences of the behavior—on what happens to the individual after he performs the act. By regulating the consequences, it is possible to reinforce behavior so that it is stamped in or to counteract it so it is extinguished.

The operant conditioning experiments were conducted by research psychologist Dr. Miriam Cohen and her colleagues in Baltimore city hospitals. The first experiment, performed with a single alcoholic patient, established the pattern; others were done with additional patients and with variations of the basic pattern.

The subject was a 39-year-old white man who had been an alcoholic for ten years. He had been hospitalized twenty times for drinking and was drinking up to two quarts a day. The longest period of sobriety in ten years was six weeks. In the two previous years he had alternated between living in his car and living in a hospital when he was drying out.

The patient was housed in a hospital ward, and a regimen was established in which he made most of the decisions about what happened to him. Everything had to be paid for, food, shelter, medication, trips to the movies, or ball games, but he could earn enough money to pay easily for everything he wanted—through good grooming and through work in the hospital laundry and in hospital maintenance. This arrangement had nothing to do with his drinking or not drinking. It served only to set up an environment in which useful constructive performance would earn him the things he wanted.

In the first experiment, lasting five weeks, the patient was told that during the first week, a "contingency" week, he had the choice of drinking up to 10 ounces of whiskey a day. If he drank 5 ounces or less, he would enjoy an "enriched" environment, which included staying in the ward with other patients, talking with the staff, having a private telephone, going to recreation room with its TV, pool table, and games, attending ward meetings, and having access to reading material. If he drank more than 5 ounces, he would be compelled to stay in an "impoverished" environment, deprived of all these privileges, and would be compelled to eat pureed food instead of a regular diet.

The second week was a noncontingency week, during which he stayed in the impoverished environment no matter how much or how little he drank. The third week was like the first (contingent), the fourth noncontingent, the fifth contingent. The question was, Would the enriched-environment contengencies reinforce a pattern of controlled drinking? The patient made a perfect score. Every day during weeks 1, 3, and 5 he drank no more than 5 ounces; every day during weeks 2 and 4 he drank the full 10 ounces.

The next question was, What would happen if the available amount of alcohol were 24 ounces—would the temptation of 24 ounces be large enough to overcome the desirability of the enriched environment and the negative effect of the impoverished environment?

The amount made practically no difference. Given the choice between drinking three-fourths of a quart of whiskey a day and losing his enriched environment, this confirmed alcoholic exceeded the 5-ounce limit only one day during the three contingent weeks. During the noncontingent weeks, he drank his full allotment of 24 ounces daily.

A repetition of these basic experiments with a number of patients produced essentially the same results, convincing the researchers that, in an experimental arrangement at least, it was possible to get a confirmed alcoholic to change to controlled drinking of small quantities of alcohol by positive reinforcement (reward) of this pattern.

Could this result be sustained over a long period of time? A new routine was established in which contingency arrangements ran for 14 days consecutively, followed by 6 noncontingent days. The alcoholics in this test stayed under 5 ounces during the entire contingency period; some even went totally abstinent during some of the contingent days and some of the noncontingent days as well.

In another variation, the positive enforcement for controlled drinking was payment in cash rather than the choice of an enriched environment. The goal was total abstinence, rather than moderate drinking. Each of the alcoholics who participated in this experiment remained totally abstinent for the reward money during the test period.

12

Treatment of Alcoholism

Any approach to the treatment of alcoholism must recognize that alcoholism does not exist by itself, that it is only one part of a personality malformation or psychiatric disorder. Whether or not the alcoholic can be successfully treated will depend in large part on the potentialities for change in the total personality—the extent to which the personality contains the resources for initiative, motivation, and control that constitute ego strength.

If the various psychiatric disorders found in association with alcoholism were arranged according to treatability, the alcoholics with the highest treatment potential would be those with neurosis, comprising about 20 percent of the total. At the other end of the spectrum would be those with severe psychosis and those with the physical and emotional deterioration of long-term, chronic alcoholism. This group, regarded as practically untreatable, comprises about 15 percent of the total.

Between the two extremes, the more treatable would be the alcoholics with passive aggressive and passive dependent personality disorders, compulsive personality, and the less severe character disorders. Among the less treatable of the middle group would be alcoholics with schizoid personality, paranoid personality, manic-depressive (cyclothymic) personality, and borderline schizophrenia.

Treatability is also evaluated in relation to age and to social, educational, and economic adjustment. The alcoholic patients who do best in treatment are those who are between 40 and 45 years of age, married, educated, occupationally skilled, occupationally stable, and free of conflict with the law.

Regardless of the specific psychiatric diagnosis, modern treatment views the alcoholic patient as a sick person with an illness he cannot handle by himself. He is recognized as a person who turned to alcohol because he could not manage without it and who then became dependent on it as a replacement for rational and realistic coping responses.

To give it up means for him a return to unendurable psychic pain without access to an anesthetic or an escape. It also requires summoning enormous measures of emotional and intellectual power to overcome a compulsion which has overpowered him and held him in thrall for so long a time. This approach recognizes the patient's suffering and problems when he is not drinking and attempts to help him find a less destructive way to deal with them.

The abstinent alcoholic is extremely uncomfortable. His intrapsychic and interpersonal conflicts continue to operate without letup, keeping him in constant distress from which he must have relief. He has learned—although the consequences have been bitter —that only alcohol gives him immediate relief. So great is the need that it will drive him to thrust aside his awareness of the disastrous results.

When he goes for help, either through the urgings of his conscience or the demands of his family or employer, he goes half wanting help, half not wanting it. Plagued by a deep feeling of aloneness, inadequacy, failure, and lack of faith in himself, he yearns for help, but his guilt, shame, and mistrust will cause him to reject the help that is offered.

A physician or psychiatrist undertaking the treatment of an alcoholic is therefore likely to be faced with a person who is hostile, obstructive, uncooperative, resistant, and insulting. The alcoholic patient will test out the doctor in many ways—by failing to keep appointments, by rejecting the doctor's advice, by provocative statements, and by starting to drink again after a few weeks' abstinence.

Seasoned clinicians anticipate such behavior and must be pre-pared to handle it with patience, tolerance, and understanding. What the alcoholic is really seeking behind his aggressiveness is a relationship of trust with someone to whom he can unburden his woes, someone to whom he can attach himself in his inordinate dependency. Whatever treatment is used, whether physical therapy or psychotherapy, the essential ingredient is the development of a relationship with the patient. The therapy cannot succeed without it. The alcoholic needs continuous and unwavering evidence that the doctor has a truly sincere interest in him.

He will reject lecturing and exhortation. He will mistrust and reject noble-sounding expressions of interest which are not matched by sincerity of action demonstrated by a willingness to go out of one's way to be helpful, by a tolerance of misbehavior and lapses, and by nonpunitive response to goading and taunting. It is not necessary to become overfriendly or overpermissive. Gentle control is regarded as the best tactic.

One of the most pervasive clinical problems, and one of the most difficult to deal with, is the patient's denial of his alcoholism and of the problems related to it. Operating on an unconscious level, the defense mechanism of denial saves the patient from the painful acknowledgment that he is sick, that he has a problem with consid-erable stigma attached to it, that he has feelings of inadequacy and low self-esteem, and that he is dependent on a drug.

The patient denies that he even has a drinking problem, let alone one as severe as alcoholism, and insists on his right to drink like anyone else. He denies the amount of liquor he has had and his inability to control his drinking. When his marriage is disrupted or his job threatened because of drinking, he deftly transfers the blame to his wife and his employer. His doctor's warnings, backed by the results of clinical tests, that his health is suffering because of his drinking are simply ignored. For every problem that develops, affecting him or his family, he develops an elaborate system of rationalization, falsification, and alibis.

Untrained practitioners trying to break through this system of denial and rationalization by means of logic and reason will find themselves hopelessly enmeshed in debate and argument, at which the alcoholic is consummately skilled. They are advised to deal with the situation objectively, without polemics, presenting to the patient the diagnosis of alcoholism together with the supporting evidence, and then to go on from there. Ultimately, when the patient feels less threatened—when the acknowledgment of alcoholism is no longer so shameful or frightening to him—he will accept his condition and work with it.

The physician may also have to reverse himself in dealing with the patient's denial as the tactical situation changes. At the beginning, the patient denies his alcoholism and insists on a psychiatric diagnosis for his problem. He is not an alcoholic, he is really neurotic or psychotic. Once the therapist has broken through this level of resistance—once the patient has accepted the diagnosis of alcoholism—the patient is likely to deny the psychiatric problem and insist on blaming all of his difficulties on his alcoholism, thus avoiding confrontation with his basic emotional difficulties.

The following chapters deal with the various categories of treatment of alcoholism: drug therapy, psychotherapy, and behavior therapy.

13

Drug Therapy

There are three distinct uses for drugs or chemicals in the treatment of alcoholism.

As chemical deterrents (such as Antabuse) they produce in combination with alcohol a violent bodily reaction. Knowledge of this reaction keeps the drinker from drinking once the deterrent has been ingested.

As psychotropic agents (tranquilizers and antidepressants) drugs are employed to counteract the agitation, anxiety, and depression found in most alcoholics and believed to play a primary role in initiating and maintaining the dependence on alcohol.

As aversive conditioning agents (such as emetine) they connect the act of drinking with a state of revulsion or fright, resulting in extinction of the drinking behavior.

CHEMICAL DETERRENTS

The chemical deterrent method, also known as chemical restraint, chemical fence, and chemical antagonizing, has been found to be one of the most effective methods in enforcing abstinence.

Antabuse

The drug most commonly used in chemical restraint treatment is Antabuse, also known by its chemical name, disulfiram. Since its introduction in 1948, Antabuse has found widespread use in private practice, sanitariums, alcoholism clinics, general hospitals, and psychiatric hospitals. It has consistently been reported to be effective in the control of alcoholic drinking.

Antabuse remains inert in the body unless alcohol is taken after it, when it produces an extremely distressing reaction: intense, throbbing headache, severe flushing, extreme nausea, vomiting, palpitations, fall in blood pressure, labored breathing, blurred vision. Anticipation of the reaction is enough, in most cases, to keep the patient from drinking after taking Antabuse. Since the Antabuse is effective for several days after it is taken, abstinence is assured for a few days, and for as long as the patient keeps taking the drug. Some physicians use the Antabuse-alcohol challenge to reinforce this abstinence. The patient is given a small amount of whiskey after he has taken Antabuse so that he will experience the sickening reaction under medical supervision. The distress caused by the reaction and the fear of its recurrence will keep him from drinking not only during the time the Antabuse is effective but often for much longer periods.

Patients taking Antabuse report that once they have taken the drug, and knowing that they can no longer satisfy their craving to drink, they find other outlets and keep themselves busy until the craving passes. The fact that the craving can be ignored and that it will go away is heartening. As therapy proceeds, the impulse to drink becomes less and less frequent. Use of Antabuse also seems to free the mind from its preoccupation with alcohol. Having made the decision to take the Antabuse, the drinker turns, without too much effort, to other things.

Many evaluation studies have been made of the effectiveness of Antabuse in maintaining abstinence.

Dr. Robert S. Wallerstein, director of a research project conducted in a Kansas Veterans Administration hospital, found that abstinence was produced with Antabuse in 53 percent of his cases, with group hypnotherapy in 36 percent, with conditioned reflex therapy in 24 percent, and with milieu therapy in 26 percent. Initially he assumed that it was the restraint alone that made Antabuse so effective, but he found that after a two-year period of abstention several of the Antabuse group started drinking again. They said that with discontinuance of the treatment routine "something had been taken away." That "something" consisted of two ingredients: the dependency relationship with the hospital and staff, and the ritual of Antabuse treatment. For patients with obsessive-compulsive personalities, ritual is an important device in repressing unconscious conflicts.

Dr. Max Hayman conducted a research test over a period of a year in an alcoholism research clinic at the University of California in Los Angeles. The unique feature was a contract which held the patient to a year's treatment. Payment was made in advance. By the end of the year 8 out of 12 patients had remained completely abstinent. Dr. Hayman expressed the belief that the commitment of patient and therapist to a full year's treatment was perhaps the most important factor. Also essential, Dr. Hayman believes, is the use of Antabuse in combination with some other treatment, preferably psychotherapy.

A group of alcoholism therapists, headed by Dr. Frederick Baekland, conducted a study of the results of a treatment of several hundred alcoholics with Antabuse in a clinic at the Downtown Medical Center, State University of New York. They found that this modality worked best with older, well-motivated, socially stable persons with compulsive personalities, the ability to form personal relationships, and relatively long drinking histories. Depressive personality, sociopathic personality, and frequent blackouts were indicators of a poor prognosis.

Reported success with Antabuse ranges from 20 to 85 percent. Though this variation might lead to skepticism, there is general agreement that this is one of the most effective measures available.

Practitioners caution against dangerous side effects from the use of Antabuse, such as psychotic episodes, suicide, and accidents. Some also list a large number of contraindications, including myocardial failure, cirrhosis, nephritis, epilepsy, goiter, pregnancy, drug addiction, asthma, and diseases of the hematopoietic (blood-forming) system. However, one of the most experienced practioners in this field, Dr. Ruth Fox, drawing on her experience with 3,000 patients, cites psychosis and decompensated heart as the only contraindications.

Temposil

Temposil, also known as citrated calcium carbamide, carbamide, and CCC, was introduced in the early 1960s as an alternate to Antabuse because it produces a less violent reaction. For several years it enjoyed the usual flurry of initial clinical reports of success, but it is only recently that any effort has been made to evaluate its effectiveness. Several studies indicate that it has a moderately successful influence in deterring drinking, and there is general agreement that it offers a suitable alternative to Antabuse, but caution is advised until there is a more exhaustive, long-term evaluation.

Metronidazole

Metronidazole is similar in its deterrent action to Antabuse and Temposil, but an additional effect is claimed for it—that it reduces the desire for alcohol. Those taking it are also said to show an improvement in their interpersonal relations, attitude toward responsibility, and behavioral symptoms. Since this drug is relatively new and has not yet been subjected to controlled, long-range studies, specialists urge a cautious evaluation of the enthusiastic claims made for it.

THE PSYCHOTROPIC DRUGS

Although the tranquilizers and, to a lesser degree, the antidepressants have been effective in treating the acute toxic condition caused by excessive intake of alcohol, they have not yet proved to have much value in treating the chronic condition—alcoholism itself. Their effectiveness has in general been limited to the control of such symptoms as anxiety, depression, tension, hallucinations, agitation, and delusions. This is the consensus of available evidence.

Yet one piece of research, conducted by Dr. Benjamin Kissin and Dr. Arthur Blatz at the Downtown Medical Center of the State University of New York, has produced indications that the psychotropic drugs may yet prove to be effective in the treatment of alcoholism. This investigation included seven separate studies, involved 1,550 patients, and covered nine years of research. The purpose was to test the effectiveness of a number of different tranquilizing and antidepressant drugs, separately and in combination. The test of effectiveness was either total abstinence or a dramatic reduction in frequency and quantity of drinking, together with a marked improvement in psychological well-being, for a six-month period following the end of treatment. The six-month period was chosen because numerous other studies have shown that the majority of relapses occur within the first six months after treatment. Those who remain abstinent or improved for that amount of time generally stay that way for five years or longer.

No single tranquilizer or antidepressant drug was found to meet the criteria for effectiveness, but one combination did prove effective—the combination of chlordiazepoxide, a tranquilizer, and imipramine, an antidepressant. The high rate of improvement for this combination, the investigators said, "is at least encouraging and it seems reasonable to hypothesize that such a combination proved more effective than either drug alone since alcoholics are typically both severely anxious and depressed. Nevertheless, our results . . . can only be considered as encouraging and require further validation."

They also discussed the theory behind the use of the tranquilizing and antidepressant drugs: "Since alcoholism is generally regarded as a psychogenic disorder, the dynamic rationale for drug therapy becomes clear. If psychotropic drugs can reduce these tensions (anxiety, depression, repressed hostility) the need to drink may be diminished or fully controlled."

Earlier studies, they note, showed that the drugs improved the psychological well-being of the patients but did not prove very effective in reducing the drinking. This, they say, may have resulted from the broadside use of one particular drug or another for all the patients in the group. Instead, the patients should have been sorted out according to their predominant psychological state (agitated depression, retarded depression, agitation, and hyperactivity) and the appropriate drug prescribed for each condition.

To illustrate, they reported that in one study thioridazine, a tranquilizer, was more effective than imipramine, an antidepressant, in the treatment of agitated depressed patients, and that in another study amitriptyline, an antidepressant, was superior to perphenazine, a tranquilizer, with retarded depressed patients.

The drugs emetine, apomorphine, and succinylcholine are used as aversive conditioning agents in the treatment of alcoholism. Since aversive conditioning is a distinct method of treatment, and since it also employs agents other than drugs, the use of emetine and the other two drugs is discussed under "Aversive Conditioning" in chapter 15.

14

Psychotherapy

Psychotherapy, a form of treatment based on psychoanalytic theory, is used almost universally in the treatment of alcoholism, in private practice as well as in the clinic and hospital. Although sometimes employed by itself, it is more commonly used in combination with some other form of treatment, such as chemical deterrent therapy or aversive conditioning therapy.

PSYCHOANALYTIC THEORY

The theoretical basis of psychoanalytic therapy is succinctly described by Dr. E. M. Blum and Dr. R. H. Blum: "The cornerstone of 'classic' psychoanalytic treatment is the assumption that unconscious conflicts that cannot find expression in socially approved activities cause mental illness (the individual suffers) or delinquent behavior (the environment suffers). The patient is unaware of unconscious conflicts that determine his conduct, influence his moods, and frequently prevent him from achieving his conscious aims. When he is under the sway of an inner need that is unconscious because it cannot be accepted, he must act in accordance with it even if it will not give him the greatest satisfaction in the long run.

"One aim of psychoanalytic treatment is to make the unconscious conscious—that is, to enable the patient to take stock of his motivations, to liberate himself from blind obedience to forces within, and to return to himself the capacity of deliberate choice. Self-knowledge is the prerequisite of choice, and choice lies in inner freedom; freedom from having to repeat habitual and unsuccessful or painful behavior patterns; freedom to direct his life insofar as this is possible; and freedom to exert mastery over his own actions. Choice implies foresight and strength enough to wait it out until alternatives have been weighed, consequences assessed, and plans made according to his ability to endure the risk and results, including the effect on others. Psychoanalytic treatment attempts to bring about the growth necessary for facing reality within and without and clearing away the obsolete, the forgotten, and the repressed by the scrutiny of old problems and the discovery of new solutions."

Psychoanalysis

In psychoanalysis (and other forms of psychotherapy deriving from it) the basic method involves a verbal and emotional interchange between the patient and the therapist. The patient's troubling feelings are probed and analyzed in an attempt to trace them back to their origins, to find out what caused them to develop as they did, to understand them in the light of past experiences. This requires tapping thoughts and emotions long repressed from consciousness and unavailable to conscious recall.

One method used to tap unconscious memories is free association, in which the patient speaks out anything that comes to mind, even if it sounds like nonsense. This method is capable of bringing into consciousness long-forgotten fears, hurts, and angers. Another method is dream analysis. Although dreams appear to be jumbled, nonsensical, and meaningless, they are full of hidden meanings which give important clues to the repressed thoughts and emotions. People in dreams are disguised versions of the key people in the patient's life—mother, father, sisters and brothers, the psychoanalyst, the dreamer himself. The things which the "characters" in the dream say and do are disguised expressions of feelings that the dreamer cannot admit to himself. With the help of the analyst, he tries to penetrate the disguises and to recognize what, underneath, he really thinks and feels.

As the digging and probing touches on sensitive areas and threatens to bring to the surface very painful feelings, the repressing forces spring back into action to thwart the exposure, causing the patient to block. His mind goes blank and he is unable to think of anything to say. This process is known as resistance. Resistance also takes other forms—forgetting treatment appointments or coming late for them; inability to bring to mind other than routine subjects for discussion; discontent with the psychoanalyst or psychoanalysis as a whole. The psychoanalyst helps the patient to recognize he is evading the real issues and works with him in overcoming the resistance.

As the psychoanalytic process continues, the patient reacts to the analyst as though he were the mother or father of his infancy, venting on the analyst the strong feelings which he had for these key people in his life. This is called transference, a crucial phase in the psychoanalytic process. As the transference proceeds, the patient reenacts with the psychoanalyst (the "parent") the original conflict of childhood, but now, in the present, he finds that the parent does not punish, does not reject, does not stifle, does not impose guilt as did the true parent.

The emotions forbidden in childhood—hate, hostility, dependency, greed, love—can now be felt without the need for repression. Once accepted and expressed they lose their power to generate the symptoms of mental illness, and the symptoms disappear.

In the process the individual truly gives up the persistent, exaggerated cravings of infancy—for protection, for mastery, for dependency, for boundless sensual gratification. Instead, he expresses himself and relates to other people in terms of mature, adult desires and needs.

In the course of psychoanalysis the patient works his way through steps and phases of personality development which were thwarted and held back in infancy and childhood because of stressful interrelationships with the mother and other key adults. What occurs in psychoanalysis is a long-delayed process of maturation.

Psychoanalytically Oriented Psychotherapy

Psychotherapy may use psychoanalytical methods without the intensity and depth of true psychoanalysis. The goals of this type of psychotherapy are to strengthen and perhaps reshape the personality, but not necessarily to rebuild it as in psychoanalysis. Psychoanalytically oriented psychotherapy does not attempt to bring about reenactment of the conflicts and emotional struggles of childhood. It does attempt to bring about the expression of repressed emotions through free association and dream analysis, but it is more concerned with the emotions being repressed in connection with the immediate situations than those repressed in childhood.

The patient is helped to see that his present way of relating to other people and the handling of his conflicts with these people are exaggerated, distorted, and inappropriate. Then he is helped to shape more effective, appropriate ways.

Supportive Therapy

Supportive therapy strives to relieve the patient of his symptoms by giving reassurance, confidence, and emotional support. The therapist acts in the role of protective parent and mentor, permitting the patient to lean on him to the fullest extent for a sense of safety and human warmth. The patient is relieved for the duration of supportive therapy of the necessity to make important decisions while the therapist gives him advice and even assistance in handling his practical problems. Supportive therapy provides a period of dependency during which the patient obtains relief from the intensely disturbing emotions which beset him—anxiety, guilt, shame, loneliness. Supportive therapy may also be used on a long-term basis with patients who are almost continually on the edge of emotional crisis and who need continuous support.

There are some patients whose ego is so fragile that they cannot tolerate the unearthing and disclosure of repressed emotions. Supportive therapy serves for these patients to keep the unacceptable emotions safely repressed and supplies them with strength from the outside to maintain internal emotional equilibrium.

Group Therapy

In group therapy, the patient interacts not only with the therapist but with other patients as well. In this setting the patient brings into play a larger range and variety of emotions than he would with the individual therapist. A degree of transference occurs not only toward the therapist but also to the other patients in the group. Other key figures besides the therapist emerge—patients who are seen as resembling a brother, sister, father, or another important person in a patient's life.

The contemporary view of group therapy is that the group serves as the "family of origin" and that the patient works through all the conflicts and problems of childhood with the surrogate parents and siblings in the group.

Group therapy and individual therapy are frequently used in conjunction. In private sessions, the therapist explores with each patient, in greater depth and on a much more intimate individual basis, the personality facets and problems which come into play in group sessions.

Group therapy often (especially in the treatment of alcoholics) makes use of a special technique called psychodrama. The patients are asked to dramatize, as though they were on stage, a scene concerned with a key emotional problem. In the process of dramatization the patient is likely to be freed of his self-consciousness and conscious control and is thus able to tap hidden emotions and conflicts. He also has the opportunity, in the safety of the group, to try out different types of roles and character portrayals which he might have been afraid to chance in real life.

RELATION OF ALCOHOLISM TO OTHER SYMPTOMS

Whichever approach is used, all psychotherapy for alcoholics attacks the drinking problem apart from and in addition to the psychiatric illness which may have produced it. This treatment of a symptom distinguishes psychotherapy in alcoholism from psychotherapy with other disorders. In the treatment of neurosis or psychosis, the symptom itself is disregarded, on the assumption that it is an indirect expression of an underlying emotional problem and that it will disappear when the emotional problem has been resolved.

Therapists working with alcoholics, however, recognize the drinking as a problem which must be handled directly, by itself, above and beyond the handling of the underlying psychological illness. Therapists continually keep before the patient the fact that he is in a difficulty and in treatment because he has a problem with alcohol. Confrontation emphasizes to the patient the destructiveness of his behavior and the effect it is having on himself and others.

Early in the psychoanalytic study of alcoholism, the distinction was made between primary, or essential, alcoholics and secondary, or reactive, alcoholics. The primary alcoholics are those who begin drinking early in life and quickly develop into full-blown alcoholics. The underlying psychiatric illness is that of character disorder. Patients with character disorder are observed to have poor motivation for cure; to be narcissistic, impulsive, cruel, greedy, and selfish; to have great need for affection and recognition, low self-esteem, a sense of helplessness and isolation, an impatient need for immediate gratification, and an inability to tolerate frustration. They display a tendency to rely on fantasy and illusion instead of realistic handling of problems.

These patients are also regarded as having poor ego development, resulting in their low capacity to control impulsive urges and behavior. They are low in internal resources (coping skills) when called upon to deal with ordinary problems of living, especially when confronted by major difficulties, losses, or failures.

They resort to alcohol early in life and quickly become dependent on it, since it offers immediate pleasure and gratification, immediate relief from frustration and mental distress, a fantasy solution to problems, an illusion of importance and success, a sense of power to overcome feelings of helplessness, a feeling of being wanted and liked, and a means of overcoming feelings of aloneness and of relating to others.

The patient with character disorder is regarded as suffering from a maldevelopment of personality and arrest of emotional growth (fixation) at an early maturational stage.

Psychoanalytic therapy is never used with alcoholics diagnosed as having a character disorder. The treatment most often used is supportive therapy and group therapy to initiate maturational processes by providing external structure and direction so that the patient will internalize both the structure and the direction and will achieve thereby the inner strength necessary for socialization and control. In the process, the ego is strengthened and coping skills developed so that the resort to alcohol is no longer the only alternative.

The secondary alcoholic is one whose alcoholism develops later in life—in his thirties or forties or even later. This type of alcoholic is generally diagnosed as neurotic. Such a patient, with fairly strong ego and good coping skills, has generally made a relatively good adjustment in life, with good work and educational history, fairly good marital history (for at least a substantial part of his life), and little or no history of trouble with the law.

These adjustments have, however, been made under great strain and at a very high cost in emotional energy. The neurotic patient suffers almost constantly from low-level anxiety and depression and often from compulsive and phobic patterns which have been integrated into what is seen as normal living. Neurotics are generally able to find sufficient satisfaction and gratification in life and to win sufficient approbation, recognition, attention, and affection to balance their anxiety, depression, and other distressing mental states. Because they are so constantly under internal stress and tension, however, they are subject to being thrown off balance (caused to regress) by sustained and intense emotional duress. When the psychic distress can no longer be endured, alcohol offers quick relief. Occasional relief drinking becomes gradually more frequent until complete psychological dependency develops.

With the neurotic patient, therapists use either classical psychoanalysis or psychoanalytically oriented psychotherapy. This approach is designed to help the patient deal with his emotional problems and resolve whatever conflicts are creating his neurotic condition. Resolution of the conflicts and enhancement of maturation reduce the anxiety and depression, the sense of inadequacy and low self-esteem, and the sense of being overwhelmed which had brought on the need for alcohol and the ultimate dependence on it.

The patient with psychosis is regarded, for treatment purposes, as a primary alcoholic. Supportive treatment is designed not only to provide him with structure and direction, which, it is hoped, he will internalize, but also to help improve his reality contacts and his ability to distinguish between what is going on inside himself and what is going on in the outside world.

FAMILY THERAPY

Individual psychotherapy emphasizes the intrapsychic (that is, internal) nature of the disorder. The illness is seen as the result of an unresolved conflict in infancy (resulting in psychoneurosis) or arrest at an early level of emotional development (resulting in character disorder or psychosis). The illness is generally dormant or only weakly manifested during the sheltered years of childhood, but when the stresses of adolescence, sexual relationships, marriage, and work are brought to bear on the individual's vulnerability the psychiatric disorder erupts in full force.

Family therapy, on the other hand, looks not at the individual patient but at the system in which he is operating, that is, his family. His sick behavior is seen, not as stemming mainly from himself, but rather as a reaction to the pushes and pulls of all other parts of the system—his relationships with the members of his family.

In families where there is great emotional tension, anger, fear, and resentment, survival groupings will form, pitting themselves against each other or against one individual in particular. It never takes this crude form openly; generally, it is couched in the softer words and feelings which people use to hide from themselves their less admirable characteristics—expressions such as "this is for his own good," or "she brought it on herself," or "everyone has to look out for himself." Regardless of the words in which the behavior is couched, it results in the isolation, helplessness, and ultimate breakdown of the victimized individual—the scapegoat.

Under the circumstances it does not do much good to treat just the sick individual, for whatever gains are made in the individual therapy sessions are broken down at home. Should he improve and escape from the family trap, the pressure will shift to another scapegoat. The problem is seen as a sick situation rather than a sick individual. The mutually destructive patterns operating throughout the family have to be broken. This is done by bringing the entire family into therapy. They meet with the therapist in different combinations: the whole family together, the mother and father alone, each of the parents alone, the children alone, the children with one or two parents, and so on.

The interlocking strangleholds are broken up and each individual is helped to operate more freely and independently, on the basis of more mature, less fearful, and more generous instincts. The freer and less frightened each one becomes the less is his need to punish another member of the family. The sick individual, relieved of his victim role, grows stronger and becomes free of his illness. The other members no longer have a need to find a victim.

This is achieved by opening up communications and permitting the free expression of fears and resentments without the threat of punishment. The scapegoating is brought to light and each person is made aware of his role in the game. Self-discovery and the enhancement of sensitivity make each person aware of the effect he has on the others and give him a guide for change. If the father or mother or one of the children has been pushed into a position of inferiority and isolation, the family is asked to concentrate on remedying the situation. Where interaction has been dominated by criticism and ridicule, the members are asked to try a more constructive way of dealing with each other.

When there is alcoholism in a family, the victim is seen as the alcoholic and therapy is directed in part toward changing the interactional patterns which keep him in this role. Efforts are also made to enhance the alcoholic's maturation so that he will not need to accept a victim's role or to use alcohol as a coping device. He is helped to deal with reality problems directly and to face them regardless of the anxiety and fear. When he no longer feels the need to face life—inside his family and out—as a victim, others will no longer be able to treat him as one.

Family therapists recognize that by the time the family with an alcoholic seeks help the alcoholism is so well established that it is necessary to deal with it by itself, in addition to dealing with the family's interactional problems. In most cases, the alcoholic is referred for separate treatment at a clinic where he may receive drug therapy; many therapists refer their patients to Alcoholics Anonymous.

15

Behavior Therapy

Since behavior therapy modifies behavior by psychological means, it is by definition a form of psychotherapy; however, it differs so distinctly from traditional types of psychotherapy that it is best to consider it in a separate category. Traditional psychotherapy concerns itself with the underlying emotional causes of the disorder. Its approach is dynamic—to get at the conflicts responsible for the pathology and to resolve them, on the presumption that when the conflict is resolved the symptom will disappear. Behavior therapy deals with the symptom directly. The symptom is regarded as learned maladaptive behavior, which can therefore become un-learned, or extinguished, through a variety of conditioned reflex techniques.

These techniques are described here according to their most common uses in alcoholism therapy and research.

AVERSIVE CONDITIONING

In aversive conditioning, a noxious stimulus, such as electric shock or a drug which produces vomiting or other bodily upset, is paired with the taste, smell, sight, and thought of liquor. The aversion originally produced by the noxious stimulus is transferred to the liquor so that from then on any reminder of the liquor will produce an aversive reaction.

Aversion-Producing Drugs

Drugs, especially the nausea- and emesis-producing drugs emetine and apomorphine, are used more than any other aversive agent in the treatment of alcohol. The drug is given first, producing nausea. A few seconds before the vomiting occurs, the patient takes a small swallow of whiskey or other liquor. The vomiting-aversion is thus transferred to the liquor, resulting in liquor aversion.

The treatment is repeated for several days. The patient is hospitalized during treatment and released when it is completed. He returns several times for reinforcement sessions.

Pioneers in this treatment are Dr. Frederick Lemere and Dr. Walter G. Voegtlin of the Shadel Sanitarium in Seattle and Dr. Joseph Thimann of the Washingtonian Hospital in Boston. At both institutions individual and group psychotherapy is an essential adjunct in the treatment program. It is assumed that conditioned reflex aversive treatment will take care of the drinking habit itself while the psychotherapy deals with the underlying emotional causes. Doctors Lemere and Voegtlin followed 4,000 of their patients over a 13-year period and found that 51 percent had remained abstinent. Dr. Thimann followed 245 patients for seven years and also found that 51 percent of his patients had remained abstinent, a remarkably similar outcome.

Occasionally Antabuse is used as the aversive agent. This is quite distinct from the use of Antabuse as a deterrent, as described in chapter 13. When it is employed as a deterrent, drinking is prevented on a day-to-day basis by the knowledge that a drink will produce a violent reaction. When Antabuse is used as an aversive agent, the patient actually takes a drink of liquor after having had a dose of the drug. The severe bodily reaction establishes a conditioned aversion to alcohol.

Experts urge caution in the use of Antabuse for this purpose since it has been known to produce severe side reactions including psychotic episodes, suicide, and myocardial infarction.

Electric Shock

In one method utilizing shock therapy, the patient is given his favorite drink and asked to sip it without swallowing it. As he does this, he receives a shock from an electrode attached to his forearm. He can rid himself of the shock by spitting out the drink. This process is repeated, but with each step the strength of the shock is increased.

In another method, the patient is seated before a display of alcoholic and nonalcoholic beverages. He is then asked to take a mouthful of whatever drink he chooses. If he chooses an alcoholic beverage, he is given a shock by an electrode attached to his forearm. If he chooses a nonalcoholic drink, he escapes the shock.

In a variation of this method, picture slides of bars, cocktail lounges, parties, and other drinking scenes are substituted for the actual sipping experience.

Apnea

The induction of apnea, a very brief paralysis of the breathing muscles, is another form of trauma used in aversion conditioning for alcoholism. When succinylcholine (Scoline) is injected into the circulatory system, it produces a frightening paralysis of breathing for about forty seconds. When the first evidence of paralysis appears, a bottle of whiskey or some other liquor is presented for the patient to see, smell, and taste. The process is repeated several times until the aversive reaction is produced by the alcohol itself. This method is still in its experimental stages.

Hypnosis

Because the use of drugs and electric shock presents many technical problems, there are attempts to achieve the same end by hypnotizing the patient into thinking he is being given an electric shock or being nauseated by a drug. A hypnotized patient is given a posthypnotic suggestion that he will experience nausea and vomiting a second after he has taken a drink. After he is awakened from the hypnosis, he is given a drink and promptly vomits. The aversive connection is established in ten or twenty sessions, followed by reinforcement sessions several months later.

Verbal Suggestion

Another substitute for the aversive agent (shock or drugs) is verbal suggestion, or covert sensitization. The patient is told to imagine himself taking a drink and the second the glass touches his lips to imagine himself violently nauseated, vomiting into the glass, over himself, over his companions. He is then told he can free himself of this revolting feeling by imagining himself pushing the liquor away, running out into the fresh air, and running home for a shower. After several such treatments, the patient is instructed to practice this sequence by himself at home and to resort to it every time he feels like taking a drink.

Although there have been claims of up to 50 percent success in obtaining long-term abstinence with electric shock aversion, breathing paralysis aversion, hypnotic aversion, and verbal suggestion, the clinical and research evidence is so scant that it is impossible to make a valid judgment.

DESENSITIZATION
AND RECIPROCAL INHIBITION

Behavior therapists have made extensive use of desensitization and reciprocal inhibition in the treatment of neurotic disorders and behavior problems such as sex deviance, compulsive eating, and phobias. It is now coming into use in the treatment of alcoholism, on the theory that the person who becomes an alcoholic has used alcohol to obtain relief from intense anxiety generated by low self-esteem and extreme discomfort in interpersonal relationships. To be rid of the alcoholism he must be rid of the anxiety.

Desensitization is achieved in the therapeutic setting by contriving a hierarchy of anxiety-provoking situations—the first designed to elicit just a little anxiety, the next a little more, the third even more, and so on. The patient is exposed to one situation at a time until he can handle even the most threatening of them.

Reciprocal inhibition consists of pairing the painful emotion (anxiety) with a pleasurable state of mind which effaces or inhibits the pain, ultimately extinguishing it.

Tom L. was admitted for treatment of alcoholism at the age of 21, when he was consuming considerably more than a quart a day. He had been drinking from the age of 16, first lightly, then quite heavily. His consumption took a sharp jump at the age of 19, when his fiancée left him.

Investigation showed that from early childhood on he had had great difficulty in meeting and conversing with people—first in school, then in social and business situations. At each new encounter he would blush, perspire, stammer, and become tongue-tied.

As the first step in desensitization he was helped to achieve total relaxation. This is standard procedure in desensitization-reciprocal inhibition therapy and can be done through relaxation training, hypnosis, or injection of a relaxing drug. In this case, hypnosis was used. He was then asked to imagine himself speaking to a friend or relative. If this created anxiety, he could put it out of his mind, think of something pleasant, and relax (reciprocal inhibition). He could then try it again until he could imagine this conversation without experiencing anxiety (desensitization). This achieved, he was asked to move on to the next step—to imagine himself talking to two friends or relatives, then three, four, and so on up to twenty, allowing him at each step to counteract his anxiety by thinking some pleasurable thought and relaxing. Strangers were then added to the imaginary group until he could tolerate talking to many strangers. Finally the assemblage was diminished, step by step, until he could tolerate talking to one stranger alone. When this was achieved, treatment was complete.

As early as the fifth or sixth treatment, Tom L. reported he was finding it easier to meet and speak with people in real life. By the twenty-third and final session, he was entirely free of anxiety in interpersonal relations. His drinking had also fallen off dramatically. In a follow-up interview 15 months later, he reported he was drinking at most one or two glasses of beer a day.

Psychologists using this method in the treatment of alcoholism say that it is not an uncommon occurrence that many patients are not only freed of alcoholism but are able to take up moderate drinking again.

Relaxation to induce reciprocal inhibition is used not only in combination with desensitization but also in combination with aversive shock therapy. It is believed that the shock eliminates the drinking response while the relaxation extinguishes the anxiety which gives rise to the drinking. Dr. George Blake, a Scottish psychologist, reports that in an experiment in which he used shock with and without relaxation, shock conditioning produced abstinence in 25 percent of his patients and reduced drinking in 27 percent. Shock and relaxation combined produced abstinence in 46 percent and in 13 percent reduced drinking.

Operant conditioning, a form of behavior therapy, extinguishes a behavior by modifying the consequences. Continuation of the behavior is punished. Abandonment of the behavior is rewarded.

The theory of this method and studies supporting it have been discussed in chapter 11.

OUTCOME OF PSYCHOTHERAPY

Measuring success by total abstinence or reduced drinking on follow-up of a year or more after treatment, success rates for psychotherapy, including behavior therapy, have been reported as being between 25 and 75 percent; when all the available evidence is evaluated critically, however, the success rate comes to about 35 to 40 percent.

In 1974, Dr. Chad E. Emrick, a psychologist at the University of Colorado, reported the aggregate findings of 271 separate studies covering several thousand patients. A third of those treated by psychotherapy were found to be abstinent on follow-up; one-twentieth had reverted to controlled drinking. In a later report (1975) covering 384 studies, Dr. Emrick found that the success rates were about the same regardless of the particular type of psychotherapy used. He also found that as many patients became abstinent without treatment as with treatment. However, reduction in the amount of drinking was much greater for the treated than the untreated patients.

16

Alcoholics Anonymous

It is the experience of clinicians specializing in the treatment of alcoholism that more alcoholics have regained sobriety through Alcoholics Anonymous than through any other method. The widespread professional endorsement of this organization is a testimonial to its effectiveness. Many practitioners refer their patients for membership in AA quite early in the treatment program. Many clinics and hospitals have an AA group operating within the facility permanently.

An excellent account of the philosophy and operation of Alcoholics Anonymous is given by Marty Mann, founder of the National Council on Alcoholism, in her *New Primer on Alcoholism.* AA is a "loosely knit, voluntary fellowship of alcoholics (and alcoholics only) gathered together for the sole purpose of helping themselves and each other to get sober and stay sober." It is not involved in any movement to combat or restrict the use of alcohol in general. "AA, as such, espouses no causes, even causes designed to help alcoholics. It does not sponsor or support hospitals, nursing homes, or sanitariums for alcoholism." This policy does not, however, restrict its individual members from becoming involved in community activities or services concerned with alcoholism. AA members are often leaders of such activities.

There is only one condition for membership in AA—the desire

to stop drinking. Membership is never solicited. The request for help needs to come voluntarily. "They wait until the alcoholic himself asks for their help—and when he asks, it is given unstintingly." Help will include "playing detective, doctor, nurse, policeman, and constant companion, giving understanding and sympathetic help at all hours of the day or night, helping out with family problems, sometimes even asking the alcoholic to live with them." There is an unyielding principle, however, that this help is given only at the request of the alcoholic, never at the request of a family member, friend, employer, clergyman, or other person.

A prospective member may find his way into AA through the suggestion and invitation of a friend who is already a member or he may make his own contact by calling a phone number or visiting an address listed in local directories.

Most newcomers to AA have a sponsor. It may be the friend who has introduced the new person to the organization, or it may be an AA member who comes to see him after he has phoned for help. From his sponsor, and later from his attendance at meetings, he learns that he is suffering from "a disease which is an obsession of the mind coupled with an allergy of the body." It is acknowledged that *allergy* may not be the correct medical term and that it is used broadly to refer to bodily susceptibility which makes the alcoholic react differently than other people do to alcohol. He learns from direct observation of the many recovered alcoholics in AA that it is possible to control the obsession, but he is warned that he can never drink again, that there is no true cure for alcoholism. His condition is likened to that of the diabetic who can control his illness with insulin even though he is not cured of it.

The "twenty-four-hour plan" advises the alcoholic that he does not need to be concerned with the long-term problem and that he should be concerned only with abstaining that day. When one day of successful abstention follows another and another, the alcoholic experiences a growing sense of self-control, achievement, and mastery, which motivates him further.

As soon as feasible, the sponsor will take his "prospect" to a meeting. There are two kinds of AA meetings. The open meeting is open to everyone, including the alcoholics' friends or relatives

and interested professional people. The audience does not participate in open meetings. There is a leader and several speakers. Each
speaker identifies himself as an alcoholic and tells about his drinking experiences, how AA has helped him, and about his recovery
and the way it has benefited him and his family. At the end of the
meeting coffee is served, and the newcomer may strike up numerous acquaintances or make dates for further social contacts—
which are invaluable as a continuing support in the struggle to
break the hold of alcohol. He is encouraged to continue to attend
meetings at least once a week.

The closed meeting is restricted to alcoholics. At closed meetings there is full audience participation, with free discussion in
which the newcomer may obtain information and help with his
problems. It too is followed by a period of socializing.

On admission to AA the new member is introduced to the AA
guidelines, known as the twelve steps, and encouraged to follow
them at his own pace:

1. We admitted that we were powerless over alcohol—that
   our lives had become unmanageable.

2. Came to believe that a Power greater than ourselves could
   restore us to sanity.

3. Made a decision to turn our will and our lives over to the
   care of God as we understand Him.

4. Made a searching and fearless moral inventory of ourselves.

5. Admitted to God, to ourselves and another human being
   the exact nature of our wrongs.

6. Were entirely ready to have God remove all these defects
   of character.

7. Humbly asked Him to remove our shortcomings.

8. Made a list of all persons we had harmed and became
   willing to make amends to them all.

9. Made direct amends to such people wherever possible except when to do so would injure them or others.

10. Continued to take personal inventory and when we were
    wrong, promptly admitted it.

11. Sought through prayer and meditation to improve our conscious contact with God as we understood Him, praying only for knowledge of His will for us and the power to carry that out.

12. Having had a spiritual awakening as a result of these steps, we tried to carry this message to alcoholics and practice these principles in all our affairs.

Psychiatrists explain the effectiveness of AA by pointing out that it undercuts the mechanisms of denial ("I am not an alcoholic"), projection ("Everybody hates me and thinks I am bad"), and rationalization ("This isn't as bad as everybody makes it out to be; I just have to have a drink now and then so I can handle all the pressures I'm under"). In Alcoholics Anonymous, the alcoholic is confronted with the seriousness of his problem in all its realistic implications and is expected to admit outright he is a helpless alcoholic. Then the responsibility for doing something about it is thrown back to him without any possibility of evasion. He is made to acknowledge the flaws in his character and to correct them through concrete acts. In the process he forms a new self-image.

In AA there is fellowship and acceptance, personal concern, and unqualified support. Members' convictions are reinforced as they introduce new members to the AA principles.

Psychoanalytic interpretation views the alcoholic as a child whose yearning for a dependency relationship with his mother has been thwarted. AA is seen as the good and loving mother who has been lost, and membership constitutes reunion with her. In the nonjudgmental, protective, and embracing role of AA there is the promise of nurture, love, care, and help.

In her article "How a Therapist Can Use Alcoholics Anonymous," Dr. Joan Curlee, psychologist at the Veterans Administration Hospital in Indianapolis, points out that the central problem of the alcoholic is the use of alcohol as an avoidance mechanism. The process is cyclical: problems lead to drinking, which creates more problems, which lead to more drinking, and so forth. The best way to break the cycle, says Dr. Curlee, is to block avoidance behavior, that is, to guide the alcoholic into a situation in which he can no longer resort to drinking and in which he is compelled to deal with his problems realistically. This, she says, is precisely what happens in AA, where total abstinence is an absolute requirement. The alcoholic also learns there that anxiety and other painful feelings are bearable and that there are better ways of dealing with life's difficulties than by drinking. As he sees others who have succeeded in giving up drinking, he recognizes that he can do it, too. As he is forced into interpersonal relationships with other AA members, he establishes a network of friends and a new support system, which counters his isolation and improves his self-esteem.

The AA group serves as a microcosm of the patient's broader social universe and reflects his basic interpersonal problems. In a setting in which he is accepted uncritically, it is possible for him to work through his problems and, with the help of the therapist, to cultivate more suitable and satisfying kinds of interpersonal behavior. Even if he is rebuffed in this experimentation, he learns in this accepting environment that he can experience rejection without falling apart and without needing to resort to alcohol.

While there is considerable acceptance of AA among psychiatrists, psychologists, and social workers involved in the treatment of alcoholics—and to a lesser extent among nonpsychiatric physicians—there is still considerable conflict between members of AA and members of the helping professions. Many AA members believe there is no place for professional services in the rehabilitation of alcoholics except for medical management in the acute phase, that "AA is enough." They also believe they have an influence with alcoholics, a nonverbal communication, which nonalcoholics and non-AA members cannot have. "Only an alcoholic can understand another alcoholic." Their emphasis on "hitting bottom" before recovery can begin also brings them into conflict with the professional.

There is especially sharp difference between AA and the psychiatric and allied professions on the role of psychotherapy and the role of drugs in the treatment of alcoholism. AA members complain of having had unsatisfactory contacts with psychiatrists and other mental-health workers. Also, some members of AA cannot accept the premise that there is an underlying psychiatric condition in alcoholism.

Use of drugs, in fact the entire notion of alcoholism as a condition which can be treated medically, runs counter to the original AA belief that alcoholism is "an allergy of the body" which cannot be corrected and that there is only one way to deal with it, the AA way: to give yourself over to "a Power greater than ourselves" and then to develop responsibility for and control over your own behavior.

The AA concept that the alcoholic is a "different type of person" has tended to thwart rational psychotherapeutic efficacy. It also tends to isolate the alcoholic, as a person, and to isolate alcoholic facilities from other medical, health, and welfare facilities in the community. Furthermore, the view of some AA members that AA is the *only* method has handicapped the development of community facilities. "If AA is enough," city and state officials say, "why do we need clinics and hospitals?" Nevertheless, the conflict is ameliorating, and there is growing evidence of mutual confidence and reciprocal help.

17

Treatment of Acute Alcohol Intoxication

The patient coming to medical attention in a state of acute intoxication is generally a very sick person in need of immediate treatment. He may be suffering not only from the immediate effects of a large intake of alcohol—"alcoholic poisoning"—but also from alcohol withdrawal. Various associated physical and mental disorders may also be present, some of immediate origin, others the products of long years of heavy drinking.

Acute alcohol intoxication may be manifested either by agitated excitement or by coma. In the case of the former, the patient manifests ataxia, slurred speech, flushed face, and combativeness. Coma is characterized by pallor, loss of reflexes, muscular relaxation, shallow respiration, and fall of blood pressure. The state of coma is regarded as a medical emergency, since death may ensue through depression of respiration if it continues.

The withdrawal syndrome may be manifested in a number of characteristic patterns:

Acute brain syndrome: The elements are confusion, dulling of the senses, and psychomotor agitation (severe shakes). There are no hallucinations.

Acute hallucinosis: Auditory hallucinations are the chief element; there may also be visual, tactile, and olfactory hallucinations.

Delirium tremens: The characteristic elements are constant tremor and intensely vivid auditory and visual hallucinations. The patient is "out of contact" and has little awareness of his surroundings. There is severe agitation and restlessness, with almost continuous motor activity. Racing pulse, profuse perspiration, and fever are also present.

The least severe of these three states is the acute brain syndrome. If it is not treated, it may progress to hallucinosis, and then to delirium tremens.

The withdrawal syndrome may occur long before the end of the drinking episode; it may begin as early as the first or second day. Symptoms usually begin during sleep, when blood concentration of alcohol is falling. Even though the withdrawal symptoms at this stage are usually mild, hallucinosis and even convulsive seizures may occur. These symptoms disappear as further drinking reestablishes a high enough blood level to repress them.

Neurological complications may be found along with or following acute intoxication:

Polyneuropathy: Involvement of sensory and motor nerve endings produces irritability, pain and itching, and loss of control of the limbs.

Korsakoff's syndrome: There is a general impairment of the thought processes, confusion, loss of sense of time and place, and a tendency to re-create memories from fantasy rather than from reality.

Wernicke's syndrome: The symptoms are disturbed functioning of vision, memory loss, confusion, wandering of the mind, stupor, and sometimes coma.

While these disorders come to attention in connection with acute intoxication, they occur only after years of heavy drinking. Korsakoff's and Wernicke's syndromes are much less common than polyneuropathy.

Physical complications frequently found in association with

acute intoxication are cardiac strain, gastritis, hemorrhage of the esophagus, liver damage, pancreatitis, emphysema, diabetes, and pneumonia.

While the treatment of acute alcohol intoxication and alcohol withdrawal varies from situation to situation, an almost standardized formula has emerged: initial administration of a tranquilizing drug; polyvitamin therapy with a heavy concentration of vitamin B; intravenous and oral administration of fluid to counteract dehydration (where necessary); maintenance of proper electrolyte balance (sodium, potassium, magnesium); a high-protein, high-carbohydrate diet.

Prior to the advent of the psychotropic drugs, such medications as paraldehyde and barbiturates were the only ones available for the treatment of the acute toxic conditions. These have now largely been replaced by the tranquilizers, which in most cases eliminate the agitation and high state of tension in a matter of hours.

Various types of tranquilizing drugs have been evaluated by recent studies:

Benzidiazepines: Chlordiazepoxide (Librium) and diazepam (Valium). These are the drugs of choice in the treatment of acute alcoholism. They also have anticonvulsant properties.

Phenothiazenes: Chlorpromazine, promazine, perphenazine, trifluoperazine. These are also effective in the treatment of acute alcoholism.

Meprobamate: Miltown or Equanil. This drug, too, is useful in the treatment of acute intoxication. It tends to become addictive, however, and also produces depressive reaction in combination with alcohol.

The antidepressant drugs are seldom used in treating the acute condition, although they have been found useful in reducing anxiety and depression as an adjunct in treating the chronic condition. The drugs most frequently referred to are amitriptyline (Elavil) and imipramine (Tofranil).

18

Treatment Facilities

In recent years, there has been a considerable increase in the kinds and numbers of facilities available for the treatment and rehabilitation of the alcoholic: inpatient, outpatient, and domiciliary.

STATE MENTAL HOSPITALS

The major inpatient facility for treatment of alcoholism is the specialized alcoholism ward in the state mental hospital. There are some private alcoholism hospitals but these handle only a small percentage of all cases.

In the past the state mental hospital was the dumping ground for patients with advanced alcoholism, sent there because there was no other place to send them or because they were also suffering from a psychosis. Little was done there for these patients beyond detoxification. A decided change has taken place, and today most state mental hospitals have specialized alcoholism wards with programs designed to treat the chronic condition, that is, the alcoholism itself.

Contrary to popular belief, the alcoholic patients in the alcoholism wards of the mental hospitals are not Skid Row types but rather members of the middle and lower-middle class, selected for admission because of factors predictive of treatability—family stability, good work history, a place in the community, good ego strength and motivation. The alcoholism treatment program in most state mental hospitals consists of these basic ingredients:

The therapeutic community: Rigid authoritarian staff structure is abandoned and all staff members are part of a therapeutic team.

Lectures and films: Didactic films and lectures are given dealing not only with alcoholism but also with physiology, psychology, and human relations.

AA meetings: There are several AA meetings a week on and off the hospital grounds.

Group therapy: In some hospitals group therapy sessions are held several times a week. Infrequently there is also individual psychotherapy for selected patients.

Occupational therapy: In many hospitals there are supervised occupational therapy programs preparing the rehabilitated patient for work in the community.

The average stay is three to eight weeks. The staff includes physicians, psychiatrists, nurses, social workers, psychologists, and psychiatric aides. In some hospitals AA is in charge of organizing the programs as well as following up on the patient after his return to the community.

ALCOHOLISM REHABILITATION HOSPITALS

There is a small number of private hospitals devoted exclusively to the treatment and rehabilitation of alcoholic patients. The program and regimen in some of these hospitals is very much like that of the alcoholism wards in the state mental hospitals, with the addition in some cases of drug treatment (psychotropic drugs and Antabuse) and greater emphasis on psychotherapy.

There is another type of private alcoholism hospital which rejects the "sick role" model (except for the treatment of acute intoxication and withdrawal on admission) and regards alcoholism as a personal problem which can be dealt with by the alcoholic himself together with the assistance of others who have been through the experience and are committed to help him. An example is the Hazelden Foundation in Minnesota. The orientation is nonmedical, and former alcoholics, trained as counselors, make up the bulk of the staff. Basic lectures on alcoholism are given, followed by group discussion. Instead of group therapy there is group counseling, aimed at understanding and dealing with the problem of alcoholism rather than insight and correction of the underlying emotional disorder. AA meetings and family sessions are an important part of the program. The programs emphasize personal responsibility and individual involvement, with reliance on cognitive control ("As you understand alcoholism you can control it") and strong group identification. Some of these hospitals have alumni programs so that after discharge the patient can keep contact with the therapeutic program. The stay in these hospitals is from three to six weeks.

AVERSION CONDITIONING HOSPITALS

Aversion (conditioned reflex) therapy, whether electric shock or chemical, is a complex, highly technical procedure requiring very close medical, nursing, and psychological supervision. It is conducted almost exclusively in special hospitals set up for this purpose, which are few in number.

Patients who are not suffering from acute intoxication are admitted directly to the long-range treatment program, which consists of an initial fixed period of hospitalization (between six and eight weeks) during which the patient receives the aversion therapy interspersed with individual and group psychotherapy sessions.

For several months after discharge from the initial hospital treatment the patient returns for follow-up treatment; this includes a number of spaced, brief readmissions to the hospital (average 36 hours) for reinforcement of the aversive conditioning. It also includes weekly or biweekly psychotherapy sessions—individual, group, and family—given in the hospital's outpatient clinic.

Patients in acute intoxication or withdrawal are first admitted to the acute treatment section for several days. They are then transferred to another section for about 10 to 14 days, to recover. This interim period is used to modify the patient's resistance and denial and to develop motivation for rehabilitation and extended treatment. He then goes into the aversion conditioning program.

GENERAL HOSPITALS

Since the acutely intoxicated person is unquestionably sick, sometimes seriously so, it would be assumed that the general hospital would admit him routinely for treatment. Yet until recently few general hospitals would admit the sick alcoholic except on referral by a physician, and then only under a disguise diagnosis such as gastritis, malnutrition, or dehydration. This practice has begun to give way under the persuasion of the American Hospital Association, and most general hospitals are admitting alcoholics openly for treatment of acute intoxication and withdrawal. A few have gone further, introducing basic alcoholism rehabilitation programs, including a combination of educational, group, and socialization activities, together with hospital work assignments and AA meetings.

A few have undertaken programs which go beyond the basic formula. The Johns Hopkins Hospital in Baltimore, for example, has developed a comprehensive alcoholism service, including facilities away from the hospital and resembling in scope the community mental health center. A patient in a state of acute intoxication or withdrawal is admitted and treated in the emergency room. If there are other medical complications requiring hospitalization, the patient is transferred to a medical ward. After the acute phase of the illness has been handled and recovery is under way, the patient is assigned to an alcoholism counselor who attempts to persuade him to enlist in the hospital's alcoholism recovery program. This includes a "quarterway" house for continued medical care combined with intensive counseling; a "halfway" house, or residential facility, to provide the recovering alcoholic with a sheltered environment; a counseling center, which operates as an outpatient service providing individual and group counseling as well as medical supervision for patients taking Antabuse; and a community center, which is a walk-in facility providing informal counseling and recreation. The community center also operates as an outreach service providing educational programs on alcoholism for schools, business firms, employee groups, and others.

Another expanded alcoholism rehabilitation program developed by a general hospital is the Alcoholism Rehabilitation Unit (ARU) in Bethesda Naval Hospital. It serves as a model for 15 similar units in Navy hospitals, all part of an overall Navy alcoholism rehabilitation program. Patients (naval personnel) are admitted either from the hospital's detoxification unit or from a waiting list on which they are placed after detoxification.

The six-week inpatient program consists of individual counseling, Antabuse, films, lectures, group discussion, AA meetings five nights a week on and off the hospital grounds, transactional analysis (a form of psychotherapy in which the patient learns about the "games" he plays in dealing with himself and other people), role-playing sessions, and occupational therapy. If a patient's family is living on or near the base, the patient and key family members come in for group discussions with other patients and their families. There is discussion of psychological and interrelationship problems.

All alumni of the ARU program living near the hospital return biweekly for a ninety-minute counseling session and for renewal of Antabuse and other medication.

OUTPATIENT ALCOHOLISM CLINICS

Outpatient clinics for alcoholics came into being in the 1950s and have since become a major modality in the treatment of alcoholism and the rehabilitation of alcoholics. There are now several hundred. Many are attached to general hospitals, making them immediately available for patients treated for acute intoxication, but admission is not limited to hospital patients or to patients in the state of intoxication; it is open to the community. Others are operated by family agencies, health departments, welfare departments, religious agencies, and private voluntary organizations.

Most community mental health centers treat alcoholics together with other psychiatric patients, making no differentiation. Some have separate units for the treatment of alcoholism.

There are several basic patterns of treatment in outpatient alcoholism clinics:

1. Didactic education (films and lectures); individual, group, and family counseling.

2. The same, together with psychotropic drugs, deterrent drugs (Antabuse), or both.

3. Psychotherapy as the core modality. These clinics, too, fall into subgroups:

    a. those combining supportive therapy with drugs (psychotropic and/or aversive). Clinics operated by physicians and nurses are likely to follow this pattern.

    b. those concentrating on individual, psychoanalytically oriented psychotherapy, and, in some cases, psychotropic drugs. These are likely to be run by psychiatrists.

    c. those concentrating on psychoanalytically oriented individual, group, and family psychotherapy, in combination. These are likely to be under the direction of psychologists and social workers.

    d. those giving behavior therapy, among other psychotherapeutic measures. These are likely to be found in the community mental health centers.

The psychotherapy-centered clinics are highly discriminatory in their intake, admitting, in the main, patients who are psychology-oriented, that is, those who are verbal, capable of insight, highly motivated, and who possess good ego strength. Family history and social, educational, and occupational assets are also considered.

These clinics have a dual goal: control of the drinking and alteration of the patient's life style and personal relationships toward a more mature level. While concentrating on the underlying or complicating psychiatric disorder, they place equal and separate emphasis on the drinking behavior itself. They do not expect that the drinking will go away by itself as the psychological condition improves.

PRIVATE TREATMENT

Many psychiatrists and some nonpsychiatric physicians treat patients with alcoholism in their private practice. So do some psychiatric social workers and psychologists who do private psychotherapy.

The nonpsychiatric physician will rely largely on counseling as well as psychotropic drugs. The psychiatrist will rely mainly on psychoanalytically oriented individual psychotherapy and family therapy, as will the social worker and psychologist.

INFORMATION AND REFERRAL CENTERS

The local councils on alcoholism, affiliates of the National Council on Alcoholism, took on, early in their history, the important functions of providing information and educational materials on alcoholism to the public at large and to health, welfare, educational, and correctional agencies. In addition they assumed the function of referring individuals or families to community facilities for rehabilitation, treatment, medical care, and health and welfare services. In recent years many have also added counseling, diagnosis, screening, and even short-term treatment. In a few cities the Alcoholism Information and Referral Center serves as the screening agency for those applying to the community's alcoholism clinic; in others it does the screening and diagnosis for the county committing courts.

The professional competence of these centers varies with the professional training of their staff. In some the staff consists mainly of recovered alcoholics, members of AA who have had no professional training; these centers are little more than referral centers for AA. There are many, however, which have full complements of professionally trained psychologists, social workers, and alcoholism counselors.

HALFWAY HOUSES

The concept of the halfway house originated in psychiatric hospital care. A halfway house for psychiatric patients is a residential facility in the community where a patient, after discharge from the mental hospital, can stop over for several weeks, or even months, to receive social, medical, and vocational rehabilitation assistance in preparation for full return to his life in the community.

In alcoholism rehabilitation, only a few halfway houses resemble the psychiatric halfway house in respect to professional programs and affiliation with such professional agencies as hospitals, clinics, and health or welfare agencies. The rest, serving an admirable purpose, and working quite effectively, are places where an alcoholic who is at a critical point in his developing alcoholism can come for friendship, emotional support, and direction in stopping his downward slide and make an attempt to reestablish himself in his family, job, and community. These are better known as recovery houses.

Several hundred recovery houses exist in the United States, most of them concentrated on the West Coast. The typical recovery house is a converted large, old home with accommodations for between ten and a hundred beds, in single and double rooms. They are operated in most cases by individuals or by organizations with deep humane concern for the alcoholic, providing him with a rehabilitation service that does not involve hospitalization. These individuals or organizations are in most cases strongly influenced by AA, and many of the managers are recovered alcoholics and AA members.

These facilities do not permit themselves to be used as drying-out stations, nor do they accept the Skid Row level of transient alcoholic. The occupants are referred by welfare departments, churches, AA, the police, courts, and word of mouth. The clientele is from the middle and lower-middle class, people with a generally good social history but who are unemployed because of their drinking.

Occupants work in the maintenance of the house and pay for their board whenever they can. All are expected to find work after initial recovery. Many who cannot are supported through welfare payments. The average stay is from a few weeks to sixty days.

The no-drinking rule is absolute, and those who break it are expelled immediately. Some recovery houses require 24 to 72 hours' sobriety before admission. Except for church-affiliated recovery houses, all make extensive use of AA. There are usually several AA meetings a week on the premises and several others off premises.

An extremely important role is played by the recovery house manager, who not only operates the house but also gives leadership as well as personal counseling on alcoholism and other matters. Authoritarian control, rigid enforcement of the rules, a strict anti-alcohol culture, and a peer relationship are regarded as key factors in helping the alcoholic achieve sobriety.

A few of the recovery houses have intramural professional therapy groups directed by social workers, psychologists, or therapeutically trained clergymen. Some have ties with therapeutic agencies and require their residents to attend alcoholism clinics.

There are special recovery houses operated by the Salvation Army in Skid Row areas, called Harbor Light agencies. They are dormitory residences, with kitchens, dining rooms, and residential facilities. The Harbor Light program is divided into two parts: the off-the-street feeding program and the residence program. The residence program resembles that in other recovery houses except that religion takes the place of AA. AA may not operate on Harbor Light premises, although Harbor Light residents may attend AA meetings elsewhere. Religion and salvation are the therapeutic modality.

Residents are expected to work in house maintenance at first, and then to find work on the outside. The Harbor Light helps them to find menial work, such as delivering telephone books and distributing handbills. As in other alcoholism recovery houses, sobriety is an absolute requirement.

The Harbor Light recovery houses maintain connections with city hospitals and clinics for medical care for their residents.

The Salvation Army has recently begun to establish Harbor Light agencies in non-Skid Row areas, placing less emphasis on rehabilitation through prayer and more on restoration of dignity, self-respect, and social status.

19

The Alcoholic Employee

In the past, the problem of the alcoholic employee was handled in only one way—the employee and his condition were ignored until they could be ignored no longer, and then he was dismissed. Today, progressive management recognizes the waste in dismissing a trained, skilled worker, as well as its responsibility to help an employee with a drinking problem as it would an employee with any other illness. Modern occupational alcoholism programs are directed toward early detection and intervention, as opposed to last-hour salvage.

Under the aegis of the National Council on Alcoholism, a joint labor-management committee has worked out a basic occupational program on alcoholism. The key to the program is the principle that alcoholism on the job cannot be detected by such obvious signs as drinking, drunkenness, accidents, and absenteeism since they may not appear in the early stages, when intervention is most effective, or the alcoholic may be very careful to conceal them.

Furthermore, giving the foreman or supervisor the responsibility of detecting and dealing with alcoholism requires of him professional knowledge and skill which he should not be required to have.

The most reliable indicator of developing alcoholism is deteriorating work performance as evidenced by unaccountably reduced quality and quantity of output; spasmodic, irregular production;

putting off of tasks; frequent mistakes; and errors in judgment. The most effective way to detect an employee with developing alcoholism is to monitor job performance. Not only is deteriorating performance a reliable indicator, it is also one the foreman or supervisor is competent to recognize and evaluate. While it may be caused by many other types of emotional or physical disorders, 50 to 65 percent of cases of deteriorating performance are related to alcoholism. Using it as a screening device for alcoholism also makes it possible to identify employees with other problems and refer them for help.

When the performance of a formerly good worker is observed to be deteriorating, he is summoned for an interview with his supervisor. He may have his union representative present if he wishes. He is told he is being called in for poor performance and is offered a referral to a counseling agency which can determine the nature of his problem and send him for treatment if necessary. There is no mention of alcoholism.

If the offer is accepted, the referral is made. If it is rejected, the worker is permitted to return to his job without further ado, but monitoring of his performance continues. If the work problem persists, he is called in for another interview and told that since his work has not improved, action must be taken. He is given the choice of accepting a referral to the counseling agency or facing disciplinary action for poor job performance. Faced with the possibility of demotion, reduction in pay, loss of seniority, or even dismissal, most workers accept the referral. Companies report the recovery of between 60 and 80 percent of the employees who go for counseling and treatment.

In addition to the step-by-step procedure for detection and referral, the management-union program on alcoholism also requires that there be in each corporation or plant a clear, written statement of policy, joined in by union and management, outlining the company's program and assuring the worker that the program is intended not to punish but to help. The statement should further assure the employee of confidentiality and of the protection of his rights and privileges of employment. Where this program is put into effect, treatment for alcoholism is covered by medical insurance.

The creators of this plan also advise that a company-wide management-union committee be established to supervise the program, and that if there is more than one plant, similar committees be set up in all.

Employers or labor unions interested in establishing an occupational alcoholism program should contact the National Council on Alcoholism. A team of consultants is assigned by NCA to meet with company and union representatives and to work out with them a set policy and procedure for the plant or company.

While the occupational alcoholism program has been designed for the limited purpose of identifying and helping the employee who is becoming an alcoholic, it has potentialities as a universal screening device for the identification of all employed persons who are becoming alcoholics, and for early intervention to prevent the further progression of their alcohol dependency. The occupational situation is uniquely suited to this type of screening and intervention.

Psychiatrists and others working with alcoholics know that the alcoholic will not give up his drinking until the forces operating in opposition to the compulsive need to drink are more powerful than the need itself. For most men (and some women) the job is pivotal to all their other relationships and to their own self-esteem. If the job is threatened, everything else is, too; hence the threat of a loss of job may do more to get the alcoholic to mobilize his resources for positive action than will almost anything else.

Industrial specialists suggest that the strategy of constructive confrontation be made part of a company's policy. Confronting an alcoholic with a crisis while he still holds a job can exert considerably more influence in getting him to mobilize his resources to stop drinking than can other pressures which come after he has already sustained the loss of job and family and no longer cares.

20

An Overview

On the basis of scientific knowledge and reasonable hypotheses, it is possible to compose a rather clear picture of alcoholism and of the alcoholic.

Alcoholism is a dependence on alcohol, primarily psychological, as a result of which the affected individual drinks compulsively to intoxication and does so repetitively and chronically. Only a small proportion of drinkers become alcoholics. Those who do are alcoholism-prone, not by virtue of a physiological defect or vulnerability specifically related to the physiological action of alcohol on the body, but rather by a predisposition to the psychological effects of alcohol on the mind and emotions. The psychological effects of alcohol are the production of instant pleasure, quick and easy relief from psychic distress, the creation of illusions pleasing to the drinker, and the modification of reality so that the drinker does not have to deal with it.

There are two basic conditions which predispose an individual to these psychological effects. One is an unremitting burden of psychic distress made up of anxiety, depression, guilt, shame, resentment, unexpressed anger, a sense of aloneness, and low self-esteem. The other is a cluster of personality traits which limit the individual's capacity to deal realistically with his emotional and practical problems. These traits are low tolerance for frustration and suffering, poor impulse control, the need for immediate gratification, and poor coping skills (low ego strength).

The psychic distress and cluster of psychological traits which make an individual alcoholism-prone are produced in part by heredity, in part by childhood experiences. Childhood experiences contributing to these conditions are instability of the family, loss of one or both parents early in life, parental conflict, parental indifference and lack of warmth, parental neglect, maternal vacillation between love and rejection (resulting in dependency conflict), lack of a clear feminine model in the mother and a clear masculine model in the father, failure to define clear sex-role expectations for the children, constant uncertainty and insecurity in the home, psychiatric illness in the parents, and antisocial deviance in the parents.

These familial influences, genetic and environmental, produce personality disturbances, often to the point of severe psychiatric illness, in the child. Within the disturbed personality structure are the components of the psychological predisposition to alcoholism.

If heavy drinking and intoxication are part of the way of life of the ethnic, religious, or social group to which the individual belongs, and if the culture fails to provide or encourage alternate ways of dealing with psychic distress and life's difficulties (such as help from family and friends, religion, psychotherapy, help from social agencies, and group support), the predisposed individual will find and take the easiest way out, that is, alcohol.

If, in addition, real life conditions are such as to cut off or shut out any possible amelioration or to offer any avenues of escape, drinking will become heavy and consistent. The relief, pleasure, and escape provided by alcohol will reinforce the drinking pattern to the point where it preempts all other possible responses.

Unless there is intervention which aborts the avoidance and escape pattern, helps the individual to strengthen his internal resources, and forces him back into realistic coping, the condition will progress and alcohol will replace the ego entirely as the integrating force of the psyche.

The time of life at which alcoholism is initiated, the speed with which it develops, the depth and extent of its progression, and the possibility of its being modified by the impact of changes in life's circumstances or by treatment depend on the basic personality structure of the susceptible individual.

People with severe character disorders or with psychoses, regarded psychoanalytically as being fixated at an early level of personality development, will take to drinking early in life, generally at the first confrontation with such problems as growing up, separating from the family, making a living, engaging in a love relationship, or "making something out of oneself." These are the primary, or essential, alcoholics. Their alcoholism starts early, develops quickly, becomes very severe, and is not very amenable to treatment.

People with less severe personality disorders and with neuroses, regarded psychoanalytically as being regressed to an earlier stage of personality development, start drinking for relief much later, generally when they are confronted with an unendurably painful trauma—the loss of a spouse, child, or parent, rejection in love, or loss of a prized position or possession. Relief and escape drinking persist if the trauma is great or if there is a chain of traumatic episodes. (Trauma is a subjective experience. What may be a disappointment or tolerable loss to one person may have the force of unendurable agony to another.) These are the reactive, or secondary, alcoholics. Their alcoholism develops more slowly, and, except at the very late stages, less intensely and deeply. The progression is protracted in these people because they have stronger coping skills and, generally, better resources for emotional support in friends, relatives, organizations, religion, or psychotherapy. They continue to call upon these internal and external resources and to struggle against the creeping enslavement of their addiction.

They are likely to come to treatment soon after they have become addicted, influenced by pressure of their family and social group, and they are likely to respond to treatment well because of still-available emotional resources.

Some will find their way out of alcoholism through spontaneous remission as the external circumstances alter and as the internal psychic distress is ameliorated by external changes or by virtue of the self-limiting nature of some anxiety, depression, tension, self-deprecation, anger, shame, and guilt.

This overview offers a realistic perspective to the problem of alcoholism and an optimistic outlook for individual alcoholics, especially for those whose condition is detected and treated in the early stages.

Concentration of public and private resources on screening for early detection and intervention, on improvement and amplification of diagnostic and treatment facilities, on training of treatment personnel, and on research to relate specific methods of treatment to specific personality configuration, psychiatric disorder, and sociocultural condition should completely change the outlook for alcoholism within the next 25 years.

Bibliography
Index

BIBLIOGRAPHY

Note: Full bibliographical information is given at first mention; thereafter author's last name and title of work, with cross reference to the first mention, are noted.

Bibliography

Introduction

Jellinek, Elvin M. *The Disease Concept of Alcoholism.* New Haven: Hillhouse Press, 1960.
———. "Phases of Alcohol Addiction." In *Society, Culture, and Drinking Patterns,* edited by David J. Pittman and Charles R. Snyder, pp. 356–368. New York: Wiley, 1962.

1. How Alcohol Affects Behavior

Greenberg, Leon A. "Intoxication and Alcoholism, Physiological Factors," *Annals of the American Academy of Political and Social Sciences* 315:22–30, 1958.
Kendis, Joseph B. "The Human Body and Alcohol." In *Alcoholism,* edited by David J. Pittman, pp. 23–30. New York: Harper & Row, 1967.
Wallgren, Henrik, and Barry, Herbert, III, eds. *Actions of Alcohol.* New York: Elsevier, 1970.

2. What Is Alcoholism?

Jellinek, Elvin M. *The Disease Concept of Alcoholism.* See listing for Introduction.

Kissin, Benjamin. "The Pharmacodynamics and Natural History of Alcoholism." In *The Biology of Alcoholism,* vol. 3, edited by Benjamin Kissin and Henri Begleiter, pp. 1–36. New York: Plenum Press, 1974.

Manual on Alcoholism. American Medical Association, 1968, p. 5.

Plaut, Thomas F. *Alcohol Problems: A Report to the Nation by the Cooperative Commission on the Study of Alcoholism.* New York: Oxford University Press, 1967, p. 39.

3. Alcoholism in Women

Beckman, Linda J. "Women Alcoholics: A Review of Social and Psychological Studies," *Journal of Studies on Alcohol* 36:797–824, 1975.

Curlee, Joan. "Women Alcoholics," *Federal Probation* 32:16–20, 1968.

Lindbeck, Vera L. "The Woman Alcoholic, a Review of the Literature," *International Journal of Addictions* 7:567–580, 1972.

Schuckit, Marc A. "The Alcoholic Woman: A Literature Review," *Psychiatry in Medicine* 3:37–43, 1972.

4. Development of Alcoholism

Jellinek, Elvin M. "Phases of Alcohol Addiction." See listing for Introduction.

Kissin, Benjamin. "The Pharmacodynamics and Natural History of Alcoholism." See listing for chapter 2.

5. Effect on Family Life

Fox, Ruth. "The Effect of Alcoholism on Children." In *Proceedings of the Fifth International Congress of Psychotherapy,* edited by B. Stokvis, pp. 55–65. Vienna: Karger, 1961.

Jackson, Joan K. "The Adjustment of the Family to the Crisis of Alcoholism," *Quarterly Journal of Studies on Alcohol* 15:562–586, 1954.

Lemert, Edwin M. "The Occurrence and Sequence of Events in the Adjustment of Families to Alcoholism," *Quarterly Journal of Studies on Alcohol* 21:679–697, 1960.

Orford, Jim. "Alcoholism and Marriage," *Journal of Studies on Alcohol* 36:1537–1563, 1975.

6. The Roots of Alcoholism

Barry, Herbert, III. "Psychological Factors in Alcoholism." In *The Biology of Alcoholism,* vol. 3, edited by Benjamin Kissin and Henri Begleiter, pp. 53–107. New York: Plenum Press, 1974.

Blane, Howard T. "Aspects of Dependency in Persons with Alcoholism," *Annals of the New York Academy of Medicine* 233:15–22, 1974.

Blane, Howard T., and Chafetz, Morris E. "Dependency Conflict and Role Identity of Drinking Delinquents," *Quarterly Journal of Studies on Alcohol* 32:1025–1039, 1971.

Blum, Eva M. "Psychoanalytical Views of Alcoholism, a Review, *"Quarterly Journal of Studies on Alcohol* 27:259–299, 1966.

Blum, Eva M., and Blum, Richard H. *Alcoholism: Modern Psychological Approaches to Treatment.* San Francisco: Jossey-Bass, 1969.

Cahn, Sidney. *The Treatment of Alcoholics: An Evaluative Study.* New York: Oxford University Press, 1970.

Goodwin, David W. "Alcohol in Suicide and Homicide," *Quarterly Journal of Studies on Alcohol* 34:144–156, 1973.

Haggard, Howard W. "Critique of the Concept of the Allergic Nature of Alcohol Addiction," *Quarterly Journal of Studies on Alcohol* 5:233–241, 1944.

Jellinek, Elvin M. *The Disease Concept of Alcoholism.* See listing for Introduction.

Jones, Mary C. "Personality Correlates and Antecedants of Drinking Patterns in Adult Males," *Journal of Consulting and Clinical Psychology* 32:2–12, 1968.

Lester, David. "Self-Selection of Alcohol by Animals: Human Variation and the Etiology of Alcoholism," *Quarterly Journal of Studies on Alcohol* 27:395–438, 1966.

Lester, David, and Greenberg, Leon A. "Nutrition and the Etiology of Alcoholism," *Quarterly Journal of Studies on Alcohol* 13:553–560, 1952.

McCord, Joan. "Etiological Factors in Alcoholism. Family and Personal Characteristics," *Quarterly Journal of Studies on Alcohol* 33:1020–1027, 1972.

McCord, Joan, and McCord, William. *Origins of Alcoholism.* Stanford, Calif.: Stanford University Press, 1960.

McCord, William, and McCord, Joan. "A Longitudinal Study of the Personality of Alcoholics." In *Society, Culture and Drinking Patterns,* edited by David J. Pittman and Charles R. Snyder, pp. 413–430. New York, Wiley, 1962.

Madsen, William. *The American Alcoholic.* Springfield, Ill.: Charles C. Thomas, 1974. See chapter 4, pp. 44–64.

Mardones, Jorge R. "On the Relationship between Deficiency of B Vitamin and the Alcohol Intake of Rats," *Quarterly Journal of Studies on Alcohol* 12:563–575, 1951.

Mendelson, Jack H. "Biochemical Mechanisms of Alcohol Addiction." In *The Biology of Alcoholism,* vol. 1, edited by Benjamin Kissin and Henri Begleiter, pp. 513–544. New York: Plenum Press, 1971.

Sherfey, Mary J. "Psychopathology and Character Structure in Chronic Alcoholism." In *Etiology of Chronic Alcoholism,* edited by Oskar Diethelm, pp. 16–42. Springfield, Ill.: Charles C. Thomas, 1955.

Smith, James J. "A Medical Approach to Problem Drinking," *Quarterly Journal of Studies on Alcohol* 10:251–257, 1949.

———. "The Endocrine Basis of Hormonal Therapy in Alcoholism," *New York State Journal of Medicine* 50:1704–1706 and 1711–1715, 1950.

Syme, L. "Personality Characteristics and the Alcoholic," *Quarterly Journal of Studies on Alcohol* 18:288–301, 1957.

Williams, R. J. "Biochemical Individuality and Cellular Nutrition: Prime Factors in Alcoholism," *Quarterly Journal of Studies on Alcohol* 20: 452–464, 1959.

Zucker, Robert A. "Sex Role Identity Patterns and Drinking Behavior in Adolescents," *Quarterly Journal of Studies on Alcohol* 29:868–884, 1968.

7. Alcohol Addiction

Curlee, Joan. "How a Therapist Can Use Alcoholics Anonymous," *Annals of the New York Academy of Science* 233:137–143, 1974.

Eddy, Nathan B.; Halbach, H.; Isbell, Harris; and Seevers, Maurice H. "Drug Dependence: Its Significance and Characteristics," *Bulletin of the World Health Organization,* no. 32, 1965, pp. 721–733.

Jellinek, Elvin M. *The Disease Concept of Alcoholism.* See listing for Introduction.

Mendelson, J. H. "Biochemical Mechanisms of Alcohol Addiction." See listing for chapter 6.

Pattison, E. Mansell. "Rehabilitation of the Chronic Alcoholic." In *The Biology of Alcoholism,* vol. 3, edited by Benjamin Kissin and Henri Begleiter, pp. 587–658. New York: Plenum Press, 1974.

Rado, Sandor. *Psychoanalysis of Behavior.* New York: Grune and Stratton, 1957.

Seevers, Maurice H. "The Psychopharmacological Elements of Drug Dependence," *Journal of the American Medical Association* 206:1263–1266, 1968.

Vogel-Spratt, M. "Alcoholism and Learning." In *The Biology of Alcoholism*, vol. 2, edited by Benjamin Kissin and Henri Begleiter, pp. 485–507. New York: Plenum Press, 1972.

WHO Expert Committee on Drug Dependence. 20th Report. WHO Technical Reports Series 551. Geneva, 1974.

8. The Influence of Heredity

Bleuler, Manfred. "Familial and Personal Background of Alcoholics." In *Etiology of Chronic Alcoholism*, edited by Oskar Diethelm, pp. 110–166. Springfield, Ill.: Charles C. Thomas, 1955.

Goodwin, Donald W., and Guze, Samuel B. "Heredity and Alcoholism." In *The Biology of Alcoholism*, vol. 3, edited by Benjamin Kissin and Henri Begleiter, pp. 37–52. New York: Plenum Press, 1974.

Goodwin, Donald W.; Schulsinger, Fini; Hermansen, Leif; Guze, Samuel B.; and Winokur, George. "Alcohol Problems in Adoptees Raised Apart from Alcoholic Biological Parents," *Archives of General Psychiatry* 28:238–243, 1973.

Goodwin, Donald W.; Schulsinger, Fini; Moller, Nils; Hermansen, Leif; Winokur, George; and Guze, Samuel B. "Drinking Problems in Adopted and Non-adopted Sons of Alcoholics," *Archives of General Psychiatry* 31:164–169, 1974.

Jellinek, Elvin M. "Heredity of the Alcoholic." In *Alcohol, Science and Society*, pp. 105–114. New Haven: Yale Center of Alcohol Studies, 1945.

Kaij, Lennart. *Alcoholism in Twins: Studies on the Etiology and Sequels of Abuse of Alcohol*, vol. 1. Stockholm: Almqvist and Wiksell, 1960.

Partanen, Juho; Bruun, Kettil; and Makkannen, Tonko. *Inheritance of Drinking Behavior*, vol. 14. Helsinki: Finnish Foundation of Alcohol Studies, 1966.

Roe, Anne. "Children of Alcoholic Parents." In *Alcohol, Science, and Society*, pp. 115–128. New Haven: Yale Center of Alcohol Studies, 1945.

Schuckit, Marc A.; Goodwin, Donald W.; and Winokur, George. "A Study of Alcoholism in Half-siblings," *American Journal of Psychiatry* 128:1132–1136, 1972.

Winokur, George; Reich, Theodore; Rimmer, John; and Pitts, Ferris N.

"Alcoholism III. Diagnosis and Familial Psychiatric Illness in 250 Alcoholic Probands," *Archives of General Psychiatry* 23:104–111, 1970.

9. Ethnic and Other Cultural Influences

Bahn, Anita K., and Chandler, Caroline A. "Alcoholism in Psychiatric Clinic Patients," *Quarterly Journal of Studies on Alcohol* 22:411–417, 1961.

Bailey, Margaret B.; Haberman, Paul W.; and Alksne, Harold. "The Epidemiology of Alcoholism in an Urban Residential Area," *Quarterly Journal of Studies on Alcohol* 26:19–40, 1965.

Bales, Richard F. "Cultural Differences in Rates of Alcoholism," *Quarterly Journal of Studies on Alcohol* 6:480–499, 1946.

_____. "Attitudes toward Drinking in the Irish Culture." In *Society, Culture, and Drinking Patterns,* edited by David J. Pittman and Charles R. Snyder, pp. 157–187. New York: Wiley, 1962.

Barchha, R.; Stewart, Mark A.; and Guze, Samuel B. "Prevalence of Alcoholism among General Hospital Ward Patients," *American Journal of Psychiatry* 115:671–684, 1968.

Barnett, Milton L. "Alcoholism in the Cantonese of New York City." In *Etiology of Chronic Alcoholism,* edited by Oskar Diethelm, pp. 179–227. Springfield, Ill.: Charles C. Thomas, 1955.

Bourne, P. J. "Alcoholism in the Urban Negro Population." In *Alcoholism,* edited by Peter J. Bourne and Ruth Fox, pp. 221–226. New York: Academic Press, 1973.

Cahalan, Don; Cisin, Ira H.; and Crossley, Helen M. *American Drinking Practices.* Rutgers Center of Alcohol Studies, Monograph no. 6. New Brunswick, N.J., 1969.

Cahalan, Don, and Room, Robin. *Problem Drinking among American Men.* Rutgers Center of Alcohol Studies, Monograph no. 7. New Brunswick, N.J., 1974.

Dozier, Edward P. "Problem Drinking among American Indians: The Role of Sociocultural Deprivation," *Quarterly Journal of Studies on Alcohol* 27:72–87, 1966.

Gorwitz, Kurt; Bahn, Anita; Warthen, Frances J.; and Cooper, Myles. "Some Epidemiological Data on Alcoholism in Maryland, Based on Admissions to Psychiatric Facilities," *Quarterly Journal of Studies on Alcohol* 31:423–444, 1970.

Hyman, Merton H. "Accident Vulnerability and Blood Alcohol Concentration of Drivers," *Quarterly Journal of Studies on Alcohol,* Supplement no. 4, pp. 34–57, 1968.

Leland, Joy. *North American Indian Drinking and Alcohol Addictions.* Rutgers Center of Alcohol Studies, Monograph no. 11. New Brunswick, N.J., 1975.

Lewis, Hylan. *Blackways of Kent.* Chapel Hill: University of North Carolina Press, 1955.

Locke, Ben Z., and Duvall, Henrietta J. "Alcoholism Among First Admissions to Ohio Public Mental Hospitals," *Quarterly Journal of Studies on Alcohol* 25:521–534, 1964.

_____. "Alcoholism Among Admissions to Psychiatric Facilities." *Quarterly Journal of Studies on Alcohol* 26: 303, 1965.

Lolli, Giorgio; Serianni, Emilio; Golder, Grace; and Luzzatto-Fegis, Pierpaolo. *Alcohol in Italian Culture.* Yale Center of Alcohol Studies, Monograph no. 3. New Brunswick, N.J.: Rutgers Center of Alcohol Studies, 1958.

McCord, Joan, and McCord, William. *Origins of Alcoholism.* See listing for chapter 6.

Maddox, George L., and Borinski, Ernst. "Drinking Behavior of Negro Collegians: A Study of Selected Men," *Quarterly Journal of Studies on Alcohol* 25:651–668, 1964.

Maddox, George L., and Williams, Jay R. "Drinking Behavior of Negro Collegians," *Quarterly Journal of Studies on Alcohol* 29:117–129, 1968.

Moon, Lewis E., and Patton, Robert E. "The Alcoholic Psychotic in New York State Mental Hospitals, 1951–1960," *Quarterly Journal of Studies on Alcohol* 24:664–681, 1963.

Morland, James K. *Millways of Kent.* Chapel Hill: University of North Carolina Press, 1958.

Robins, Lee; Murphy, George E.; and Breckenridge, Mary B. "Drinking Behavior of Young Negro Men," *Quarterly Journal of Studies on Alcohol* 29:657–684, 1968.

Sadoun, Roland; Lolli, Giorgio; and Silverman, Milton. *Drinking in the French Culture.* Rutgers Center of Alcohol Studies, Monograph no. 5. New Brunswick, N.J., 1965.

Snyder, Charles R. "Culture and Jewish Sobriety." In *Society, Culture, and Drinking,*" edited by David J. Pittman and Charles R. Snyder, pp. 188–225. New York: Wiley, 1962.

Sterne, Muriel W. "Drinking Patterns and Alcoholism among American Negroes." In *Alcoholism,* edited by David J. Pittman, pp. 66–99. New York: Harper & Row, 1967.

Viamontes, Jorge A., and Powell, Barbara, J. "Demographic Characteristics of Black and White Male Alcoholics," *International Journal of Addictions* 9:489–94, 1974.

Vitols, M. M. "Culture Patterns of Drinking in Negro and White Alcoholics," *Diseases of the Nervous System* 29:391–394, 1968.

Zax, Melvin; Gardner, Elmer A.; Hart, William T. "Public Intoxication in Rochester; a Survey of Individuals Charged During 1961," *Quarterly Journal of Studies on Alcohol* 25:669–678, 1964.

————. "A Survey of the Prevalence of Alcoholism in Monroe County, N.Y., 1961," *Quarterly Journal of Studies on Alcohol* 28:316–327, 1967.

10. The Marriage Partner of the Alcoholic

Bailey, Margaret B. "Alcoholism and Marriage: A Review of Research and Professional Literature," *Quarterly Journal of Studies on Alcohol* 22:81–97, 1961.

Bailey, Margaret B.; Haberman, Paul; and Alksne, Harold. "Outcomes of Alcoholic Marriages: Endurance, Termination or Recovery," *Quarterly Journal of Studies on Alcohol* 23:610–623, 1962.

Bowen, Murray. "Alcoholism as Viewed through Family System Theory and Family Psychotherapy," *Annals of the New York Academy of Science* 233:115–122, 1974.

Edwards, Patricia; Harvey, Cheryl; and Whitehead, Paul C. "Wives of Alcoholics: A Critical Review and Analysis," *Quarterly Journal of Studies on Alcohol* 34:112–132, 1973.

Fox, Ruth. "The Alcoholic Spouse." In *Neurotic Interaction in Marriage,* edited by V. W. Eisenstein, pp. 148–168. New York: Basic Books, 1956.

Meeks, Donald E., and Kelly, Colleen. "Family Therapy with the Families of Recovering Alcoholics," *Quarterly Journal of Studies on Alcohol* 31:399–413, 1970.

Orford, Jim. "Alcoholism and Marriage." See listing for chapter 5.

Whalen, Thelma. "Wives of Alcoholics: Four Types Observed in a Family Service Agency," *Quarterly Journal of Studies on Alcohol* 14:632–641, 1953.

11. Basic Dogmas Are Challenged

Bailey, Margaret B., and Stewart, Jean. "Normal Drinking by Persons Reporting Previous Drinking Problems," *Quarterly Journal of Studies on Alcohol* 28:305–315, 1967.

Bigelow, G.; Cohen, Miriam; Liebson, Ira A.; and Faillace, Louis A. "Abstinence or Moderation: Choice by Alcoholics," *Behavior Research and Therapy* 10:209–214, 1972.

Cohen, Miriam; Liebson, Ira A.; and Faillace, Louis A. "The Role of Reinforcement Contingencies in Chronic Alcoholism: An Experimental Analysis of One Case," *Behavior Research and Therapy* 9:375–379, 1971.

———. "A Technique for Establishing Controlled Drinking in Chronic Alcoholics," *Diseases of the Nervous System* 33:46–49, 1972.

———. "Controlled Drinking by Chronic Alcoholics over Extended Periods of Free Access," *Psychological Reports* 32:1107–1110, 1973.

Cohen, Miriam; Liebson, Ira A.; Faillace, Louis A.; and Allen, Richard P. "Moderate Drinking by Chronic Alcoholics," *Journal of Nervous and Mental Diseases* 153:434–444, 1971.

Cohen, Miriam; Liebson, Ira A.; Faillace, Louis A.; and Speers, Wendell. "Alcoholism: Controlled Drinking and Incentives for Abstinence," *Psychological Reports* 28:575–580, 1971.

Davies, D. L. "Normal Drinking in Recovered Alcohol Addicts," *Quarterly Journal of Studies on Alcohol* 23:94–104, 1962. See also "Normal Drinking in Recovered Alcoholics," special reprint in *Quarterly Journal of Studies on Alcohol* (New Brunswick, N.J.: Rutgers Center of Alcohol Studies, Publication Division, 1962). Comment on "Normal Drinking in Recovered Alcohol Addicts," with reply by Davies.

Davies, D. L.; Scott, F.D.; and Malherbe, M. E. L. "Resumed Normal Drinking in Recovered Psychotic Alcoholics," *International Journal of Addictions* 4:187–194, 1969.

Drew, Leslie R. H. "Alcoholism as a Self-limiting Disease," *Quarterly Journal of Studies on Alcohol* 29:956–967, 1968.

Goodwin, Donald W.; Crane, J. Bruce; and Guze, Samuel B. "Felons Who Drink: An 8-Year Follow-up," *Quarterly Journal of Studies on Alcohol* 32:136–147, 1971.

Gottheil, Edward; Alterman, Arthur I.; Skoloda, Thomas E.; and Murphy, Brendan F. "Alcoholics' Pattern of Controlled Drinking," *American Journal of Psychiatry* 130:418–422, 1973.

Gottheil, Edward; Corbett, Lacey; Grasberger, Joseph C.; and Cornelison,

Floyd S., Jr. "Fixed Interval Drinking Decisions," *Quarterly Journal of Studies on Alcohol* 33:311–324, 1972.

Gottheil, Edward; Crawford, Harold D.; and Cornelison, Floyd S., Jr. "The Alcoholic's Ability to Resist Alcohol," *Diseases of the Nervous System* 34:80–84, 1973.

Gottheil, Edward; Murphy, Brendan F.; Skoloda, Thomas E; and Corbett, Lacey O. "Fixed Interval Drinking Decisions II," *Quarterly Journal of Studies on Alcohol* 33:325–340, 1972.

Hyman, Merton. "Alcoholics: Fifteen Years Later." Unpublished study in preparation for doctoral dissertation, 1975.

Kendell, R. E. "Normal Drinking by Former Alcohol Addicts," *Quarterly Journal of Studies on Alcohol* 26:247–258, 1965.

Kendell, R. E., and Staton, M. C. "Fate of the Untreated Alcoholic," *Quarterly Journal of Studies on Alcohol* 27:30–41, 1966.

Lovibond, S. H., and Caddy, G. "Discriminated Aversive Control in the Moderation of Alcoholics' Drinking Behavior," *Behavior Therapy* 1:437–444, 1970.

Mello, Nancy K. "Behavioral Studies of Alcoholism." In *The Biology of Alcoholism,* vol. 2, edited by Benjamin Kissin and Henry Begleiter, pp. 219–291. New York: Plenum Press, 1972.

Mills, Kenneth C.; Sobell, Mark B.; and Shaefer, Halmuth H. "Training Social Drinking as an Alternative to Abstinence for Alcoholics," *Behavior Therapy* 2:18–27, 1971.

Paredes, Alfonso. "Denial, Deceptive Maneuvers, and Consistency in the Behavior of Alcoholics," *Annals of the New York Academy of Science* 233:23–33, 1974.

Paredes, Alfonso; Hood, William R.; Seymour, Harry; and Gollob, Maury. "Loss of Control in Alcoholism: An Investigation of the Hypothesis with Experimental Findings," *Quarterly Journal of Studies on Alcohol* 34:1146–1161, 1973.

Pattison, E. Mansell. "Rehabilitation of the Chronic Alcoholic." See listing for chapter 7.

12. Treatment of Alcoholism

Blum, Eva M., and Blum, Richard H. *Alcoholism: Modern Psychological Approaches to Treatment.* See listing for chapter 6.

Blume, Sheila B. "Psychodrama and Alcoholism," *Annals of the New York Academy of Science* 233:123–127, 1974.

Cahn, Sidney. *The Treatment of Alcoholics: An Evaluative Study.* See listing for chapter 6.

Fox, Ruth. "Treatment of Alcoholism: A Multidisciplinary Approach," *Postgraduate Medicine* 38:A106–A116, 1965.

Glasscote, Raymond M. *The Treatment of Alcoholism.* Washington, D.C.: The Joint Information Service of the American Psychiatric Association and the National Association for Mental Health, 1967.

Hayman, Max. *Alcoholism: Mechanism and Management.* Springfield, Ill.: Charles C. Thomas, 1966.

Kissin, Benjamin; Rosenblatt, Sidney M.; and Machover, Solomon. "Prognostic Factors in Alcoholism," *Psychiatric Research Reports* 24:22–43, 1968.

McDonald, Donald E. "Group Characteristics of Alcoholics," *Annals of the New York Academy of Science* 233:128–134, 1974.

Pattison, E. Mansell. "Rehabilitation of the Chronic Alcoholic." See listing for chapter 7.

"Trends in the Treatment of Alcoholism." In *Alcohol and Health,* edited by Mark Keller, pp. 111–128. Rockville, Md.: National Institute on Alcohol Abuse and Alcoholism, 1974.

13. Drug Therapy

Baekeland, Frederick; Lundwall, Lawrence; Kissin, Benjamin; and Shanahan, Thomas J. "Correlates of Outcome in Disulfiram Treatment of Alcoholism," *Journal of Nervous and Mental Diseases* 153:1–9, 1971.

Benor, Daniel, and Ditman, Keith S. "Tranquilizers and Management of Alcoholism: A Review of the Literature to 1964. Part II," *Journal of Clinical Pharmacology* 7:17–25, 1967.

Ditman, Keith S. "Review and Evaluation of Current Drug Therapies in Alcoholism," *Psychosomatic Medicine* 28:667–677, 1966.

Fox, Ruth. "Treatment of Alcoholism: A Multidisciplinary Approach." See listing for chapter 12.

————. "Disulfiram-Alcohol Side Effects," *Journal of the American Medical Association* 204:271–272, 1968.

Hayman, Max. "Treatment of Alcoholism in Private Practice with a Disulfiram-oriented Program," *Quarterly Journal of Studies on Alcohol* 26:460–467, 1965.

Kissin, Benjamin, and Platz, Arthur. "The Use of Drugs in the Long Term Rehabilitation of Chronic Alcoholism," American College of Neuropsychopharmacology, *Proceedings of the 6th Annual Meeting,* 835–851, 1968.

Kissin, Benjamin, and Gross, Milton M. "Drug Therapy in Alcoholism," *Current Psychiatric Therapy* 10:135–144, 1970.

Lehmann, H. E., and Ban, T. A. "Chemical Reduction of the Compulsion to Drink with Metronidazole: A New Treatment Modality in the Therapeutic Program of the Alcoholic," *Current Therapy Research* 9:419–428, 1967.

Lundwall, Lawrence, and Baekeland, Frederick. "Disulfiram Treatment of Alcoholism: A Review," *Journal of Nervous and Mental Diseases* 153:381–394, 1971.

Mottin, J. L. "Drug-induced Attenuation of Alcohol Consumption: A Review and Evaluation," *Quarterly Journal of Studies on Alcohol* 34:444–472, 1973.

Penick, S. B.; Carrier, Russell N.; and Sheldon, Judith B. "Metronidazole in the Treatment of Alcoholism," *American Journal of Psychiatry* 125:1063–1066, 1969.

Platz, Arthur; Panepinto, William C.; Kissin, Benjamin; and Charnoff, Stanley M. "Metronidazole and Alcoholism: An Evaluation of Specific and Non-specific Factors in Drug Treatment," *Diseases of the Nervous System* 31:631–636, 1970.

Wallerstein, Robert S. *Hospital Treatment of Alcoholism: A Comparative Study.* Menninger Clinic Monograph Series, no. 11. New York: Basic Books, 1957.

14. Psychotherapy

Blum, Eva M., and Blum, Richard H. *Alcoholism: Modern Psychological Approaches to Treatment.* See listing for chapter 6.

Blume, Sheila B. "Psychodrama and Alcoholism." See listing for chapter 12.

Bowen, Murray. "Alcoholism as Viewed through Family System Theory and Family Psychotherapy." See listing for chapter 10.

Cahn, Sidney. *The Treatment of Alcoholics: An Evaluative Study.* See listing for chapter 6.

Emrick, Chad D. "A Review of Psychologically Oriented Treatment of Alcoholism. I. The Use and Interrelationship of Outcome Criteria and Drinking Behavior Following Treatment," *Quarterly Journal of Studies on Alcohol* 35:532–549, 1974.

Esser, P. H. "Conjoint Family Therapy with Alcoholics: A New Approach," *British Journal of Addiction* 64:275–286, 1970.

Ewing, John A., and Fox, Ruth. "Family Therapy of Alcoholism," *Current Psychiatric Therapies* 8:86–91, 1968.

Fox, Ruth. "Modification of Group Psychotherapy for Alcoholics," *American Journal of Orthopsychiatry* 35:258–259, 1965.

_____. "Psychiatric Aspects of Alcoholism," *American Journal of Psychotherapy* 19:408–416, 1965.

Gallant, D. M.; Rich, A.; Bey, E.; and Terranova, L. "Group Psychotherapy with Married Couples: A Successful Technique in New Orleans Alcoholism Clinic Patients," *Journal of the Louisiana Medical Society* 122:41–44, 1970.

Haley, Jay. *Changing Families: A Family Therapy Reader*. New York: Grune and Stratton, 1971.

Minuchin, Salvador. *Families and Family Therapy: A Structural Approach.* Cambridge: Harvard University Press, 1974.

Yalom, Irvin D. "Group Therapy in Alcoholism," *Annals of the New York Academy of Science* 233:85–103, 1974.

15. Behavior Therapy

Abrams, Stanley. "An Evaluation of Hypnosis in the Treatment of Alcoholics," *American Journal of Psychiatry* 120:1160–1165, 1964.

Anant, Santokh S. "Treatment of Alcoholics and Drug Addicts by Verbal Aversion Techniques," *International Journal of Addictions* 3:381–388, 1968.

Ashem, Beatrice, and Donner, Lawrence. "Covert Sensitization with Alcoholics: A Controlled Replication," *Behavior Research and Therapy* 6:7–12, 1968.

Blake, George B. "The Application of Behavior Therapy to the Treatment of Alcoholism," *Behavior Research and Therapy* 3:75–85, 1965.

_____. "A Follow-up of Alcoholism Treated by Behavior Therapy," *Behavior Research and Therapy* 5:89–94, 1967.

Chapman, R. F.; Burt, D. W.; and Smith, J. W. "An Experimental Analysis of Human Avoidance Behavior of Alcohol," *Alcoholism* 9:87–91, 1973.

Cautela, Joseph R. "The Treatment of Alcoholism by Covert Sensitization," *Psychotherapy* 7:86–90, 1970.

Devenyi, P., and Sereny, G. "Aversion Treatment with Electroconditioning for Alcoholism," *British Journal of Addiction* 65:289–292, 1970.

Emrick, Chad D., "A Review of Psychologically Oriented Treatment of Alcoholism I." See listing for chapter 14.

――――. "A Review of Psychologically Oriented Treatment of Alcoholism II," Journal of Studies on Alcohol 36:88–99, 1975.

Franks, Cyril M. "Conditioning and Conditioned Aversion Therapies in the Treatment of the Alcoholic," *International Journal of the Addictions* 1:61–98, 1966.

Kraft, Tom, and Al-Issa, Ihson. "Alcoholism Treated by Desensitization," *Behavior Research and Therapy* 5:69–70, 1967.

――――. "Desensitization and the Treatment of Alcohol Addiction," *British Journal of Addiction* 63:19–23, 1968.

Laverty, S. G. "Aversion Therapies in the Treatment of Alcoholism," *Psychosomatic Medicine* 28:651–666, 1966.

Lemere, Frederick, and Voegtlin, Walter G. "An Evaluation of the Aversion Treatment of Alcoholism," *Quarterly Journal of Studies on Alcoholism* 11:199–204, 1950.

Madill, Mary-Frances; Campbell, Rugal; Laverty, S. G.; Sanderson, R. E.; and Vandewater, S. L. "Aversion Treatment of Alcoholics by Succinylcholine-induced Apneic Reaction," *Quarterly Journal of Studies on Alcohol* 27:483–509, 1966.

Thimann, Joseph. "Conditioned Reflex Treatment of Alcoholism," *New England Journal of Medicine* 241:368–370, 1949.

16. Alcoholics Anonymous

Curlee, Joan. "How a Therapist Can Use Alcoholics Anonymous." See listing for chapter 7.

Hayman, Max. *Alcoholism: Mechanism and Management.* See listing for chapter 12. Charles C. Thomas, 1966.

Madsen, William. *The American Alcoholic.* Springfield, Ill.: Charles C. Thomas, 1974, pp. 154–197.

Mann, Marty. *New Primer on Alcoholism.* New York: Holt, Rinehart and Winston, 1958.

Maxwell, Milton A. "Alcoholics Anonymous: An Interpretation." In *Society, Culture and Drinking Patterns,* edited by David J. Pittman and Charles R. Snyder, pp. 577–585. New York: Wiley, 1962.

17. Treatment of Acute Alcohol Intoxication

Benor, Daniel, and Ditman, Keith S. "Tranquilizers in the Management of Alcoholics: A Review of the Literature to 1964. Part I," *Journal of New Drugs* 6:319–337, 1966.

_____. "Tranquilizers in the Management of Alcoholics: A Review of the Literature to 1964. Part II." See listing for chapter 13.

Hudson, Frederick G., and McGowan, Janice M. "Outpatient Management of Acutely Ill Alcoholics," *Quarterly Journal of Studies on Alcohol* 26:680–683, 1965.

Johnson, Robert B. "The Alcohol Withdrawal Syndromes," *Quarterly Journal of Studies on Alcohol,* Supplement no. 1, pp. 66–76, 1961.

Kaim, Samuel C.; Klett, Charles J.; and Rothfeld, Benjamin. "Treatment of the Acute Alcohol Withdrawal State: A Comparison of Four Drugs," *American Journal of Psychiatry* 125:1640–1646, 1969.

Koppanyi, T. "Problems in Acute Alcohol Poisoning," *Quarterly Journal of Studies on Alcohol,* Supplement no. 1, pp. 24–36, 1961.

Lawrence, Fred E. "The Outpatient Management of the Alcoholic," *Quarterly Journal of Studies on Alcohol,* Supplement no. 1, 117–128, 1961.

Manual on Alcoholism. See listing for chapter 2.

Salzberger, Gideon J. "Treatment of Acute Alcohol Poisoning in a State Mental Hospital," *Diseases of the Nervous System* 25:293–297, 1964.

18. Treatment Facilities

Blum, Eva, and Blum, Richard H. *Alcoholism: Modern Psychological Approaches to Treatment.* See listing for chapter 6.

Cahn, Sidney. *The Treatment of Alcoholics: An Evaluative Study.* See listing for chapter 6.

Glass, George S. "Model for an Alcohol Rehabilitation Unit in a Military General Hospital." In *Proceedings of the 3rd Annual Conference,* National Institute on Alcohol Abuse and Alcoholism, DHEW publ. no. (ADM) 75-137, 1974, pp. 280–291.

Hayman, Max. *Alcoholism: Mechanism and Management.* See listing for chapter 12.

Pattison, E. Mansell. "Rehabilitation of the Chronic Alcoholic." See listing for chapter 7.

Reading, Anthony. "The Role of the General Hospital in Community

Alcoholism Programs." In *Proceedings of the 3rd Annual Conference,* National Institute of Alcohol Abuse and Alcoholism, DHEW publ. no. (ADM) 75-137, 1974, pp. 254–266.

19. The Alcoholic Employee

A Joint Union-Management Approach to Alcoholism Recovery Programs. New York: National Council on Alcoholism, 1975.

Maxwell, Milton A. "Alcoholic Employe: Behavior Changes and Occupational Alcoholism Programs," *Alcoholism* 8:174–180, 1972.

Trice, Harrison M., and Roman, Paul M. The Strategy of Constructive Confrontation." In *Spirits and Demons at Work: Alcohol and Other Drugs on the Job.* Ithaca: New York State School of Industrial Relations, Cornell University, 1972, pp. 170–196.

Index